Eating Disorders Among Athletes

Theory, Issues, and Research

David R. Black
Editor

Association for the Advancement of Health Education
and
National Association for Girls and Women in Sport

Associations of the
American Alliance for Health,
Physical Education, Recreation and Dance

Dedication

To Henry Dahna (1887–1968), my beloved grandfather, whose concerned comment about an underweight woman etched a lasting memory in my mind: "She doesn't weight more than a pound of soap after a week's wash."

Contents

iii

About the Authors

RoseAnn Benson is assistant professor, Department of Health, Sport and Leisure Studies, George Mason University, Fairfax, VA. Her doctoral dissertation (Southern Illinois University) was titled *Selected Eating Practices and Weight Control Techniques Among Elite Women Swimmers*. She has been a swimming coach for over 20 years.

David R. Black is associate professor of health promotion and education at Purdue University, West Lafayette, IN. He is an active scholar in the area of eating disorders and athletes. He has published numerous articles pertaining to weight management/eating disorders and regularly teaches a graduate seminar on this topic.

Mardie E. Burckes-Miller is associate professor of health education and health education coordinator at Plymouth State College of the University System of New Hampshire. She has published in journals such as *Research Quarterly for Exercise and Sport, Athletic Training Journal,* and *Health Education* on the topic of eating disorders and athletes and she has presented on the topic since 1982 to state, regional, national, and international audiences.

Joanne S. Chopak is a doctoral candidate in the College of Health and Human Development at the Pennsylvania State University. Previously she was a health educator at the McKinley Health Center, University of Illinois, Urbana- Champaign. Her master's thesis, titled *Eating Disorder Behaviors and Attitudes Among Female College Athletes,* served as the basis for her chapter.

Sharon R. Guthrie is an assistant professor of physical education at California State University, Long Beach. She was among the first researchers to examine eating disorders among athletes and is co-editor of a book on women in sport (in progress, Human Kinetics Publishers).

Suzanne E. Held is the coordinator of health education for the Bureau of Community Health Services, Marion County Health Department, Indianapolis, IN.

Virginia G. Overdorf is professor and chair of the Department of Movement Sciences at William Paterson College, Wayne, NJ. She was formerly the coach of a nationally-ranked Division III team at the college and was National Coach of the Year in 1984. She has written and spoken widely on the topic of eating disorders and female athletes.

Christine S. Smithies is a staff psychologist in the Department of Psychiatry, College of Medicine, University of Cincinnati, Cincinnati, OH. She works in the Eating Disorders Clinic, a treatment center for women from all over the country who have severe eating disorders. She also provides consultation for eating disordered athletes and their coaches.

Donald H. Steel is professor of kinesiology at the University of Maryland, College Park. He currently serves as advisor to the Wellness Research Laboratory in the College of Health and Human Performance and is coordinator of the sport psychology program at the university. His research interests have centered on stress and human performance.

Karen T. Sullivan is assistant professor in the physical fitness management program at Marymount University, Arlington, VA. She has written on the stress experienced by professional athletes and is examining the eating behaviors of college students as they relate to restraint and cognitive style. She has coached swim teams and served as a fitness consultant to the U.S. Department of Justice.

Mary Taylor-Nicholson is associate professor of health education at the Pennsylvania State University, University Park. She has published several articles on the topic of women's health and was the advisor to Joanne Chopak's study.

Valerie A. Ubbes is assistant professor of health education at Northern Illinois University, Dekalb. She is a certified health education specialist with research interests in health promotion and behavior change theory. She has coached numerous All-American athletes in gymnastics at the University of Southern Colorado and Ohio State University and has initiated sport nutrition education for gymnasts at NIU, USC, and OSU.

Preface

This book is the first of its kind on the topic of eating disorders and athletes. It presents an initial perspective on what may become a distinct subarea within the field of eating disorders. The book evolved in a relatively short period of time in response to an exigent request to provide important new information about a serious problem confronting athletes and the sports community.

The book originated with a "Call for Editors" published in several professional publications. Prospective editors forwarded curriculum vitae and samples of published work in the field of eating disorders and weight management. Editors were selected from a list of eligible individuals.

Articles for the book were solicited in several ways. Accompanying the call for editors was a "Call for Papers" which requested manuscripts for the special monographs on eating disorders and athletes. Investigators conducting research in this area also were contacted to inquire about their work or their students' work that would be appropriate for inclusion in the volume. Names of other colleagues who were doing interesting work were requested and these individuals were contacted too. In addition, a computerized literature search was completed of *Dissertation Abstracts International* and *Psychological Abstracts*. Potential contributors identified by this process were contacted and invited to submit chapters. Papers based on thesis and dissertation research were given special consideration for several reasons. First, the best research conducted often occurs as part of completing requirements for graduate degrees. Second, there was a desire to encourage and provide a publication opportunity to first-time authors in hopes that they might continue to publish in the future. Last, synopses from theses and dissertations are rarely published and their circulation is limited. Ultimately, the quality of the contribution determined whether it was accepted for publication, not the manner in which it was solicited or the prior experience or reputation of the author(s).

The articles for this book were selected through a long, careful screening process. Initial papers received from the Call for Papers were reviewed by at least two and as many as four reviewers. Reviewers were selected based on their familiarity with the theme of the paper. Dorothy B. McKnight, Jean Lundholm, and the editor evaluated reviewers' comments for each manuscript and then decided on the suitability of the chapter for the research volume. Authors were informed of this decision, and suggestions for revisions and reviewers' comments were provided.

Papers received by contacting authors directly received the same careful scrutiny. Papers were sent to at least two or more reviewers and suggestions were provided by the editor about revising the manuscript.

Each time a chapter was revised, it was reviewed and editor's suggestions were provided. Manuscripts ultimately selected presented new information, minimized redundancy, focused on different populations, addressed important issues, offered a new perspective, and/or were included for historical significance. It should be noted that space limitation, focused theme, and publication deadlines dictated that a number of excellent chapters had to be declined.

Contributors are to be commended for their patience and tenacity, and for enduring a demanding editor. Most every chapter went through multiple revisions. In some cases, authors rethought or refocused the themes of their papers, redid analyses, and consulted with a variety of experts to verify the accuracy of what was reported. Long distance calls often occurred between authors and the editor. Because of the short time intervals allotted for revisions, many authors incurred substantial postal expenses due to the number of overnight mailings. Substantial effort was expended by all contributors in order to produce a high quality professional product.

Reviewers were hand picked and petitioned based on diversity of expertise. Reviewers were specialists in eating disorders, sociology, physical education, health promotion and education, psychology, statistics, and combinations of these disciplines. I am extremely grateful to Ron A. Thompson for the many hours he spent in carefully critiquing papers and writing detailed reactions. I also appreciate the efforts of Mardie E. Burckes-Miller for first bringing this opportunity to my attention and freely giving of her time to review papers, often on short notice, and for her support and encouragement when the process became arduous. Daniel C. Coster's efforts should be acknowledged for providing consultation about statistical issues related to analyses. I am also indebted to the following reviewers for their thoughtful suggestions and the time they devoted: Maria T. Allison, Donald L. Corrigan, Joy DeSensi, Susanne E. Held, Jean Lundholm, Leslie G. McBride, and Kate Nelson.

Several other people were instrumental in the publication process. Dorothy B. McKnight, who was responsive and supportive throughout the entire process, was exceptionally helpful. I would especially like to thank Judy K. Black, my wife, for pitching in when the work load and time demands became overwhelming. She devoted many hours to making sure that details were communicated to contributors and offering an opinion about the best ways to communicate and convey ideas. Kim Orth spent many hours typing letters to contributors, retyping manuscripts, and arranging for overnight letter delivery which was especially appreciated. Her extraordinary efforts made it possible to meet publication deadlines.

David R. Black, Editor

1

Eating Disorders Among Athletes: Current Perspective

DAVID R. BLACK

The purpose of this chapter is to present background information that led to the publication of this first volume of empirically focused articles on eating disorders among athletes. The topic has gained national and international notoriety as society faces the unpleasant realities about the human frailties of athletes. Within the last 10 years, approximately 70 publications have appeared specifically related to eating disorders and athletes. The dangers of unhealthy attitudes, behaviors, and the use of weight loss methods may or may not be known to the athlete, but the perceived benefits may outweigh any ill effects. This book presents theory, issues, and the latest research in the area in a concise and readable form for a wide variety of audiences. The goal is to recognize eating disorders among athletes as a distinct subarea and to ultimately eliminate the problem in sport.

Eating disorders among athletes have become a major concern, which has evolved due to a number of factors related to athletes and sport performance. First, there is heightened awareness that athletes are human, not invincible, and susceptible to a wide variety of problems thought previously to be restricted to the general public. Recent media coverage has shown that athletes are vulnerable to gambling, alcohol and drug abuses, philandering, and other indulgences perceived as unlawful, immoral, or both. Second, these problems are being exhibited by both professional and amateur athletes at all levels. For example, Pete Rose was recently evicted from baseball because of gambling and Ben Johnson, the Olympian, was disqualified and his gold medal rescinded because of steroid use. Third, stellar athletes representing a variety of sports have publicly admitted how devastated they have been by eating disorders or their preoccupation with weight, dieting, and exercise. Many have spoken at college campuses and shared their experiences with others in hopes of bringing attention to the problem and preventing others from replicating their experiences. Famous athletes who have acknowledged an eating disorder include Cathy Rigby McCoy, Nadia Comenici, Mary Lou Retton, Lori Kosten, Rosalynn Summers, Kathy Ormbsy, and Mary Wazeter, to name but a few (McDermott, 1982; Moriarty & Moriarty, 1988).

Fourth, data are beginning to confirm what athletes have been indicating, that the problem is not simply isolated to a few individuals but affects many, both men and women. In fact, recent estimates suggest that college athletes are up to six times more likely than the general public to display anorexic or bulimic eating behaviors; men tend to use more aggressive unhealthy approaches to lose weight such as excessive exercise and women rely on more passive means such as fasting, self-induced vomiting, and fad dieting (e.g., Black & Burckes-Miller, 1988; Burckes-Miller & Black, 1988a, 1988b). Fifth, national organizations have recently expressed their concern about eating disorders and athletes. For example, recent actions have been taken by the American Alliance for Health, Physical Education, Recreation and Dance (AAHPERD) as well as other professional associations. The National Collegiate Athletic Association has sponsored a two-part videotape (Hand, 1989a, 1989b), the first titled "Afraid to Eat: Eating Disorders and Student Athletes" and the second, "Out of Balance: Nutrition and Weight."

History

Eating disorders among athletes have recently been addressed in the professional literature. This volume focuses on eating disorders among athletes as a separate and distinct subarea within the field of eating disorders. Heretofore, the topic of eating disorders among athletes has been enmeshed within the broader field of eating disorders. Athletes with eating disorders undoubtedly share some commonalities with the general public with eating disorders, but the context and problems pertaining to etiology, prevalence, and intervention may vary. In fact, the problem among athletes in some ways may be more complex. There are two complex phenomena to be considered, eating disorders and the world of athletics. Both are multifaceted and contain expectations about performance and achievement of societal ideals. Also, perceptions about both are largely shaped by society.

To date, there have been approximately 70 publications (excluding the 11 chapters in this volume) on the specific topic of eating disorders and athletes; almost all have been articles. The articles have been published in a vast number of journals but the largest percentage have appeared in *The Physician and Sportsmedicine, Medicine and Science in Sports and Exercise, International Journal of Eating Disorders* (since 1988), and the *Journal of Physical Education, Recreation and Dance* (19.2%, 9.6%, 6.8%, and 5.5%, respectively).

One of the first scholarly articles appeared in 1976 and was written by Nathan J. Smith, a psychiatrist. He published three other pieces that also might be considered early contributions in 1980, 1983, and 1984. Other major scholarly works began to appear as well during this time-frame and were authored by Vincent (1979, 1989), Huber (1983), and Popma (1983). A round table discussion was published in 1985 that called attention to the problem of eating disorders and athletes (Zucker et al., 1985). One of the first service oriented articles was published by Thompson (1987).

The first research studies isolated single athletic populations, and four subpopulations were most popular. One of the first pieces about dancers/ballerinas was published by Druss (1979) and another by Malo-ney (1983). Costar (1983) and Short and Short (1983) were among the first to report studies on gymnasts, and Blumenthal, O'Toole, and Chang (1984) focused on long distance runners. Wrestlers have been a unique population because of the rapid weight loss and gain phenomena typical in the sport. Problems associated with wrestlers "making weight" have been discussed by many including early publications such as those by Hansen (1978) and Tipton (1980). Another more recent subpopulation to receive attention are swimmers and an early article in this area was by Dummer, Rosen, Heusner, Roberts, and Counsilman (1987). The progression in publishing has continued and one of the first articles to focus on women in a variety of sports was written by Rosen, McKeag, Hough, and Curley (1986). Articles that have focused on both men and women athletes participating in a variety of sports have been authored by Black and Burckes-Miller (1988) and Burckes-Miller and Black (1988a, 1988b). The first doctoral dissertation on this topic was by Sharon Guthrie (1985) and is summarized in this volume.

Papers about eating disorders and athletes presented at professional meetings or conferences began to appear in the early 1980s. One of the first papers presented at an international conference was by Chipman et al. (1981). Three other papers were also presented at an international conference but not until the middle of the decade (Bauman, Comenitz, & Gibson, 1986; Burckes-Miller & Black, 1986a; Hamilton, Brooks-Gunn, & Warren, 1986). One of the first papers to be presented at a regional conference was by Burckes-Miller and Black (1986b, 1986c) and at a state conference by Burckes-Miller (1983).

Personal Effects of Eating Disorders

Some of the personal benefits and dangers of an eating disorder or a preoccupation with food and weight are presented in Table 1.1. The list of benefits and dangers is based on available literature but should not be considered comprehensive. Further research may add other factors to the list.

The personal effects of eating disorders may be formally or informally taken into account by athletes. Some athletes may only be partially aware of the consequences of engaging in pathogenic attitudes and behaviors and using unhealthy weight loss methods. Even if athletes engage in a formal decision-making process and calculate the risks, they may believe that the consequences of an eating disorder will not happen to *them* or if something bad *does* happen, it will occur in the distant future (cf. Weinstein, 1984). Athletes may often focus on the current benefits of their actions (e.g., improved athletic performance) with little regard for future consequences (e.g., personal harm) (Gardner, 1990). Consequences of their actions may be ignored in hopes of receiving immediate benefits. The perceived benefits may be even greater than those listed in Table 1.1. For example, athletes may receive recognition, fame, and fortune for maintaining an athletic appearance whether it is *healthy* or not. These are obviously powerful lures or inducements to counter the impact of ill effects. Unfortunately, the negative as well as

Table 1.1

Some Possible Positive and Negative Effects Related to Unhealthy Attitudes, Behaviors, and Weight Loss Methods

State/Condition	Description	Potential Effect
BENEFITS		
Elevated endorphins	Excessive exercise and being below normal weight releases a chemical in the brain	Elevated mood, emotional "high"
Regular exercise	Constant training and physical activity above average level	Reduced risk of coronary heart disease
Chronic caloric restriction	Routine reduction of calories	Reduced risk for certain cancers
Low percentage body fat	For women below 20–25%, for men below 15–18% (age 18)	Aesthetically appealing, improved performance

Low body weight	Below acceptable weight standards for age and height	Improved vertical movement, ease in being lifted or carried, meet weight categories
Reduced libido	Reduced sexual drive from excessive exercise and caloric restriction	Improved ability to concentrate on sport
Early exercise training	Vigorous exercise program as an adolescent or young athlete	Number of fat cells may be lower than average

DANGERS

Hypokalemia	Severe dehydration and loss of electrolytes from constant vomiting	Fainting, convulsions, cramps, heat exhaustion, decreased strength and endurance, circulatory collapse
Nutrient deficient diets	Diets lacking the required vitamins, minerals, proteins, and fat	Permanent joint, organ, and muscle damage, weakened immune system, lack of endurance and strength
Amenorrhea (women) or lack of testosterone (men)	Absence or suppression of menses in women or delayed pubic changes in both sexes	Permanent infertility, lack of mature body frame
Weight cycling	Constant weight loss and weight gain	Greater risk of hypertension
Rapid weight loss	Losing more than 2% of body weight per week	Liver damage, loss of lean tissue, electrolyte and kidney problems
Redistribution of body fat	Fat lost from one site may be regained at another (e.g., lower body, gynoid area)	Increased risk of cardiovascular disease and cancer
Lowered metabolic rate with low body weight	Caloric requirements to maintain weight are lower	Weight gained easily and difficulty maintaining normal weight

Note. This information is consolidated from the following sources: Boe (1985); Brownell, Steen, and Wilmore (1987); Chipman, Hagan, Edlin, Soll, and Carruth (1983); Falls and Humphrey (1978); Hamilton, Brooks-Gunn, and Warren (1985); Huber (1983); Romeo (1984).

the positive consequences occur whether attended to or not. Cumulative research evidence suggests that being eating disordered or engaging in behaviors that mimic an eating disorder can lead to serious physiological and psychological sequelae and even to death.

Overview

This is the first collection of empirically focused articles pertaining to eating disorders and athletes. This special volume was commissioned by the Association for the Advancement of Health Education (AAHE) and the National Association for Girls and Women in Sport (NAGWS).

Purpose of the Book

This book calls attention to eating disorders and pathogenic behaviors and attitudes among athletes as well as the unhealthy, if not unsavory, use of methods to lose weight. It presents theory, issues, and research relevant to eating disorders among athletes and discusses a sociological context of eating disorders and athletics along with current issues. The papers provide the most recent information about eating disorders and athletes, as well as suggestions for future research. The chapters are written in a concise, readable form and in a research format that allows for quick access to information. Where possible, actual research questionnaires are supplied as well as psychometric information about these new instruments. Data about athletes from single sports such as gymnastics and swimming are included as well as research regarding athletes from a variety of collegiate and noncollegiate sports. A futures article proposes a large-scale coordinated national effort to reduce or abate eating disorders among athletes.

Intended Audiences

The book is intended for those interested in the latest information about eating disorders and athletes and is appropriate reading for upper division college and graduate students as well as scholars and researchers. Other audiences include athletes, coaches, athletic trainers, team physicians, administrators, health education professionals, sport psychologists, nutritionists, specialists in eating disorders and weight management, as well as parents and others closely associated with the athlete who are trying to understand more about the problem. The readings are also appropriate as a text or supplemental text in classes that focus on issues related to eating disorders and athletes separately or in combination. The book might be considered for courses in coaching, health education, sports administration, athletic training, psychology, counseling, public health, education, nutrition, nursing, and medicine.

Perspective

Research in the area of eating disorders and athletes is continuing to grow and develop. It is hoped that this book contributes to that growth by encouraging scholarship and research. This volume may help to further consolidate efforts and to ameliorate or abate problems related to food, exercise, and body weight and participation in athletics.

The findings in this volume are in no way to be considered complete or authoritative. At some future time another volume may possibly be prepared. Feedback is welcomed about the worth and merit (i.e., the extrinsic and intrinsic value) of the book (see Guba & Lincoln, 1981). Ideas about the focus of a future volume along with information about new or ongoing research in the area would be appreciated.

References

Bauman, J., Comenitz, L., & Gibson, J. (1986, April). *An assessment of eating disorder characteristics in a marathon running population.* Paper presented at the 2nd International Conference on Eating Disorders, New York City.

Black, D. R., & Burckes-Miller, M. E. (1988). Male and female college athletes: Use of anorexia nervosa and bulimia nervosa weight loss methods. *Research Quarterly for Exercise and Sport, 59,* 252–256.

Blumenthal, J. A., O'Toole, L. C., & Chang, L. C. (1984). Is running an analogue of anorexia nervosa? *JAMA, 232,* 520–523.

Boe, E. E. (1985). The physiological and psychological consequences of excessive weight loss in athletics. *Athletic Training, 20,* 238, 240–242.

Brownell, K. D., Steen, S. N., & Wilmore, J. H. (1987). Weight regulation practices in athletes: Analysis of metabolic and health effects. *Medicine and Science in Sports and Exercise, 19,* 546–556.

Burckes, M. E. (1983, October). *Eating disorders: A problem in athletics.* Paper presented at the Nebraska Association for Health, Physical Education, Recreation, and Dance, Omaha, NE.

Burckes-Miller, M. E., & Black, D. R. (1986a, April). *Eating disorder behaviors of male and female college athletes*. Paper presented at the 2nd International Conference on Eating Disorders, New York City.

Burckes-Miller, M. E., & Black, D. R. (1986b, November). *Eating disorders and athletes*. Paper presented at the 6th Annual Society of Teachers of Family Medicine North Central Conference, Omaha, NE.

Burckes-Miller, M. E., & Black, D. R. (1986c, November). *Prevalence of anorexia, bulimia, and eating disorders behaviors among college athletes*. Paper presented at the 6th Annual Society of Teachers of Family Medicine North Central Conference, Omaha, NE.

Burckes-Miller, M. E., & Black, D. R. (1988a). Behaviors and attitudes associated with eating disorders: Perceptions of college athletes about food and weight. *Health Education Research: Theory & Practice, 3*, 203–208.

Burckes-Miller, M. E., & Black, D. R. (1988b). Male and female college athletes: Prevalence of anorexia nervosa and bulimia nervosa. *Athletic Training, 23*, 137–140.

Chipman, J. J., Edlin, J. C., Hagan, R. D., Carruth, B. R., Soll, M. H., & Eichenwald, H. F. (1981). Extreme weight-loss in the adolescent athlete: Misguided dieting or a mask of anorexia-nervosa. *Pediatric Research, 15*, 441.

Chipman, J. J., Hagan, R. D., Edlin, J. C., Soll, M. H., & Carruth, B. R. (1983). Excessive weight loss in the athletic adolescent. *Journal of Adolescent Health Care, 3*, 247–252.

Costar, E. D. (1983). Eating disorders: Gymnasts at risk. *International Gymnast, 25*, 58–59.

Druss, R. G. (1979). Body image and perfectionism of ballerinas: Comparison and contrast with anorexia nervosa. *General Hospital Psychiatry, 2*, 115–121.

Dummer, G. M., Rosen, L. W., Heusner, W. W., Roberts, P. J., & Counsilman, J. E. (1987). Pathogenic weight-control behaviors of young competitive swimmers. *The Physician and Sportsmedicine, 15*(5), 75–84.

Falls, H. B., & Humphrey, L. D. (1978). Body type and composition differences between placers and non-placers in an AIAW gymnastics meet. *Research Quarterly for Exercise and Sport, 49*, 38–43.

Gardner, R. W. (1990). *Performance enhancing substances in sport: An ethical study*. Unpublished doctoral dissertation, Purdue University.

Guba, E. G., & Lincoln, Y. S. (1981). *Effective evaluation*. San Francisco: Jossey-Bass.

Guthrie, S. R. (1985). The prevalence and development of eating disorders within a selected intercollegiate athlete population. *Dissertation Abstracts International, 46*, 3649A-3650A. (University Microfilms No. ADG86-03006, 8606).

Hamilton, L. H., Brooks-Gunn, J., & Warren, M. P. (1985). Sociocultural influences on eating disorders in professional female ballet dancers. *International Journal of Eating Disorders, 4*, 465–477.

Hamilton, L. H., Brooks-Gunn, J., & Warren, M. P. (1986, April). *The role of selectivity in the etiology of eating disorders in American and Chinese ballet dancers.* Paper presented at the 2nd International Conference on Eating Disorders, New York City.

Hand, C. (Producer). (1989a). *Afraid to eat: Eating disorders and student athletes.* (Videotape). Wilkes-Barre, PA: Karol Media.

Hand, C. (Producer). (1989b). *Out of balance: Nutrition and weight.* (Videotape). Wilkes-Barre, PA: Karol Media.

Hansen, N. C. (1978). Wrestling with "making weight." *The Physician and Sportsmedicine, 27*(4), 107–110.

Huber, S. (1983). Starving for competition. *Sports Nutrition News, 2,* 1–4.

Maloney, M. J. (1983). Anorexia nervosa and bulimia in dancers: Accurate diagnosis and treatment planning. *Clinical Sports Medicine, 2,* 549–555.

McDermott, B. (1982). Gone. *Sports Illustrated, 57*(20), 83–86, 88, 90, 92, 94, 96.

Moriarty, D., & Moriarty, M. (1988). *Socio-cultural influences in eating disorders: Focus on sports/fitness programs.* Unpublished manuscript, University of Windsor, Windsor, Ontario.

Popma, A. (1983). *Weight control: The athlete's obsession. Squash, 4*(4), 14–15.

Romeo, F. (1984). The physical educator and anorexia nervosa. *Physical Educator, 41*(4), 2–5.

Rosen, L., McKeag, D. B., Hough, D. O., & Curley, V. (1986). Pathogenic weight control behavior in female athletes. *The Physician and Sportsmedicine, 14*(1), 79–84.

Short, S. H., & Short, W. R. (1983). Four-year study of university athletes' dietary intake. *Journal of American Dietetic Association, 82,* 632–645.

Smith, N. J. (1976). Gaining and losing weight in sports. *JAMA, 236,* 149–154.

Smith, N. J. (1980). Excessive weight loss and food aversion simulating anorexia nervosa. *Pediatrics, 66,* 139–142.

Smith, N. J. (1983). Weight control and heat disorders in youth sports. *Journal of Adolescent Health Care, 3,* 231–236.

Smith, N. J. (1984). Weight control in the athlete. *Clinical Sports Medicine, 3,* 693–704.

Thompson, R. A. (1987). Management of the athlete with an eating disorder: Implications for the sport management team. *The Sport Psychologist, 1,* 114–126.

Tipton, C. M. (1980). Physiologic problems associated with the "making of weight." *American Journal of Sports and Medicine, 8,* 449–450.

Vincent, L. M. (1979; 2nd ed. 1989). *Competing with the sylph: Dancers and the pursuit of the ideal body form.* Kansas City: Andrews and McNeel.

Weinstein, N. D. (1984). Why it won't happen to me: Perceptions of risk factors and susceptibility. *Health Psychology, 3,* 431–457.

Zucker, P., Avener, J., Bayder, S., Brotman, A., Moore, K., & Zimmerman,
    J. (1985). Eating disorders in young athletes: A round table. *The Physician
    and Sportsmedicine, 13,* 88–91, 94–103, 106.

Author Notes

Mardie E. Burckes-Miller is acknowledged for her contributions to
this chapter. She provided citations and reference materials and
reviewed information presented in the historical section. She also suggested materials to consider in the description of the personal effects
of eating disorders on athletes. Her time and efforts are gratefully
appreciated.

2

College Athletes and Eating Disorders: A Theoretical Context

MARDIE E. BURCKES-MILLER

DAVID R. BLACK

This chapter presents a theoretical perspective of eating disorders among college athletes. Athletes may be influenced to a greater degree by sociological compared to biogenetic and psychological determinants. The importance of the environment is underscored and athletes are recognized as a unique subpopulation because of the seemingly disproportionate number of athletes who satisfy criteria for eating disorders, exhibit eating disorder symptomatology, and utilize pathogenic weight control methods. The specific sociological factors considered are culture, media, roles of men and women, peers, coaches and other authority figures, and family. A sociological context is presented to better understand and mitigate or abate problems related to eating disorders and athletes, to stimulate research, to identify or develop interventions to alter negative environmental influences, and to tailor treatment programs specifically to this subpopulation.

> *One can never be too thin or too rich.*
> *Duchess of Windsor[1]*

The comment by the Duchess of Windsor sums up a pervasive attitude in American culture about acceptable body standards. Undoubtedly, the Duchess of Windsor might prefer to qualify her statement if she were aware of and sensitive to the prevalence of eating disorders, especially among college athletes who are highly visible, yet susceptible and vulnerable to environmental influences. This chapter presents a

---

[1]From *The Penguin Dictionary of Modern Quotations* (2nd ed.), J. M. Cohen & M. J. Cohen (Eds.), New York: Penguin, page 360.

theoretical perspective of eating disorders among college athletes that emphasizes sociological factors. Sociological factors are defined as the influence of the environment on human behavior.

The impact of the environment seems important for several reasons. First, eating disorders are the only common type of psychopathology in which sociological variables appear to be a major factor in determining prevalence. Environmental factors may contribute to other types of psychopathology, such as schizophrenia and affective disorders, but not significantly (Mitchell & Eckert, 1987).

Further reason for a sociological emphasis is that athletes may not be as vulnerable regarding biogenetic and psychological factors as non-athletes. Because of the selection process, athletes are superior physically. There is also recent evidence that athletes may be superior emotionally. Mallick, Whipple, and Huerta (1987), for example, found that athletes were the most psychologically healthy compared to those diagnosed as eating disordered and to a group of high school and junior high school students. Athletes were superior on the psychological self subscale which included impulse control, emotional tone, and body and self-image; in terms of social self which included social relationships, morals, and vocational-education goals; family self which focused on family relationships; and coping self which included mastery of the external world, psychopathology, and superior adjustment. Athletes, however, may be more prone to eating disordered attitudes and behaviors as well as other symptoms related to anorexia nervosa and bulimia nervosa (Black & Burckes-Miller, 1988; Burckes-Miller & Black, 1988a, 1988b, 1988c). Data suggest that athletes may be part of a unique subculture but that part of this group may, in fact, be vulnerable to eating disorders. Stress related to athletic and academic performance, desire to please, and insecurities associated with attempts to comply with the expectations of others may, for example, increase the likelihood that they will engage in unhealthy behaviors that could lead to a bona fide eating disorder. Therefore, athletes' environment may have a more predominant impact compared to other determinants of eating disorders and in relation to the general public. The contention is that if the environment could be modified, the prevalence of anorexia nervosa and bulimia nervosa might be dramatically diminished among athletes.

The three determinants of eating disorders, biogenetic, psychological, and sociological, are reviewed below in accordance with the research literature relevant to athletes. The biogenetic and psychological determinants, however, are briefly reviewed. The major emphasis is on the sociological determinant. A sociological context is introduced to accomplish the following: (a) understand and mitigate or abate problems related to eating disorders and athletes, (b) identify or develop interventions to alter negative environmental influences, (c) design or modify treatment programs to meet the needs of athletes, and (d) stimulate research.

Biogenetic Factors

The contribution of biogenetic factors to the initiation and perpetuation of eating disorders is the most evident of all the determinants, but less is known about this factor than any of the others. Historically, researchers interested in identifying determinants of eating disorders thought that anorexia nervosa and bulimia nervosa occurred because of the malfunction of the pituitary gland. More recent work has examined whether the biological abnormalities found in these disorders are secondary to the effects of starvation or whether they represent some underlying, primary, pathophysiological disturbance that explains the pathogenesis of the illness (Kaplan & Woodside, 1987). Other evidence suggests that bulimia may be a variant of a depressive disorder (Strober & Humphrey, 1987) that may have a biogenetic basis.

It has been suggested that in addition to the genetic predisposition for a specific body weight, perhaps there is a genetic predisposition for an eating disorder. Research in this area is in the early stages, but initial evidence suggests inherited clusterings are associated with eating disorders. Kaplan and Woodside (1987), for example, noted several interesting points. First, athletes who have abnormal and irregular eating patterns appear to follow in their parents' footsteps, and also have altered brain neurotransmitters which change the release of the hypothalamic hormone. This hormone is important in producing normal menstruation and ovulation. Second, a reduction in body fat decreases the sensitivity of the hypothalamus to other influences that cause the hypothalamus to produce normal menstruation and ovulation. In addition, the opiods, endorphins produced in the "runner's high," have been linked to eating behaviors. Starvation, as well, has been known to increase opiod release. Finally, it has been noted that sustained and frequent exercise has been associated with amenorrhea (McArthur et al., 1980).

Psychological Factors

A number of psychological factors have been identified that may contribute to eating disorders. Psychological research on puberty has

suggested that sex differences in the impact of early versus late matura-
tion may be important in identifying risk factors for bulimia nervosa
(Striegel-Moore, Silberstein, & Rodin, 1986). Other characteristics that
have been studied concern the view that eating disorders, particularly
bulimia nervosa, are basically substance abuse disorders, with food
being one of many or the only substance abused (Wooley & Wooley,
1981). In addition, researchers have found that women who experience
more stress are at greater risk for binge eating. Stress is not an independent risk factor, but occurs in conjunction with other risk factors that
may play a role in increasing the likelihood of developing an eating
disorder (Striegel-Moore et al., 1986). Interestingly too, Olmsted and
Garner (1984) point out that bulimia and psychopathology are not necessarily connected because the majority of women they studied who had
vomited to control their weight were as well adjusted as those who had
never vomited.

Sociological/Environmental Factors

Central to an etiological analysis of eating disorders are sociological/
environmental factors. Figure 2.1 depicts the determinants of eating
disorders as three circles. Parts of the circles overlap to represent that
some factors interact and are influenced by more than one determinant.
The circles can be conceptualized as the same size but their influence
may be disproportionate. It is also recognized that all three determinants
impact the athlete even though the focus is on the sociological determinant as indicated by the shading of the biogenetic and psychological
determinants.

The sociological determinant is divided into several factors and the
athlete is placed in the center to represent the influence of each factor
on the person. Although the segments of the circle are divided equally
(or nearly so), the relative influence of each of the seven factors may
vary depending on the individual athlete. The factors listed are not
meant to be exhaustive but represent ones thought to have the greatest
influence. In addition, the factors may be applicable to or interact with
more than one determinant and apply to collegiate as well as to younger
and older female and male athletes.

Culture

While the ideal body form has varied over time and between cultures,
there is some support for the contention that the preferred shape for

women in Western cultures has shifted toward a thinner ideal over the past 20 years (Garner & Garfinkel, 1980; Mazur, 1986; Silverstein, Perdue, Petersen, Vogel, & Fantini, 1986). This is supported by the changes in accepted body type during this century from the ample mature figure in Rubens' paintings (Brumberg, 1988; Rosenzweig & Spruill, 1987) to the thin figure of Twiggy, the English model. Data from *Playboy* centerfolds and Miss America contestants from 1960 to 1980 revealed a significant trend toward a thinner standard (Garner, Garfinkel, Schwartz, & Thompson, 1980). Garner et al. also noted over this period that the contestant group in general became taller and thinner, although during the same period biological studies have shown that the population has become taller and heavier. Finally, the trend for males has paralleled the trend for women. Men strive to be lean and muscular and are influenced by the emphasis on fitness and the athletic look of models, athletes, and nonathletes alike.

There is an expectation today to live up to the fitness/sport look. For example, Moriarty and Moriarty (1988) noted that for women, fitness

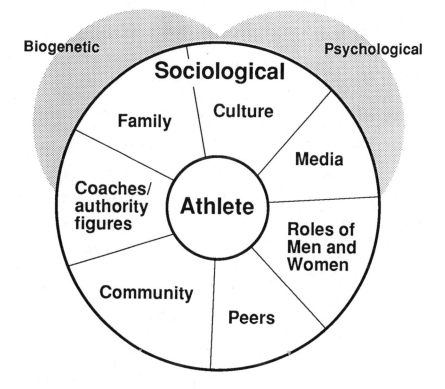

Figure 2.1. Sociological influences in athletics.

and exercise is related to weight control and, for many, a development of a curveless body shape. In conjunction with this, the authors also stated that men pursue fitness to attain certain health benefits (e.g., better cardiovascular functioning) while women predominantly pursue fitness to lose weight. This point is also illustrated by the findings of the Canada Fitness Survey (Shephard, 1986) in which only 31% of the men pursued fitness to lose weight while over 50% of the women participated in fitness for this reason.

Cultural pressures to be thin and fit also occur in formal athletics and being a winner is highly valued. The importance of winning may vary according to the level of sport or the emphasis placed on it. For example, a star basketball player at a Big Ten university might feel more pressure to win than a team player from a small state college. In some instances, superior athletic records lead directly to financial reward and employment opportunities for both coaches and players. The potential of the athlete also seems to be a factor in the pressure to succeed regardless of the personal cost. Obtaining a competitive edge has become a reality as athletic performance improves. Athletes pressured to do their best all the time may consider diverse means of acquiring a competitive edge (cf. Black & Burckes-Miller, 1988). Extreme measures of gaining an advantage may be appealing because of the perceived potential to enhance technique, physical performance, and appearance (Rosen, McKeag, Hough, & Curley, 1986). One presumed way to improve is the use of pathogenic weight control methods for the purpose of performing in lighter weight categories, increasing speed, controlling vertical movements, and improving the ability to be lifted or carried (Burckes-Miller & Black, 1988b). Concurrently, unhealthy attitudes and behaviors may develop about food and weight that may lead to a bona fide eating disorder (Burckes-Miller & Black, 1988a; 1988c).

Male and female athletes as a subpopulation appear to be more prone to eating disordered behaviors and attitudes, as well as to the syndromes of anorexia nervosa or bulimia nervosa, than members of the general population. For example, Burckes-Miller and Black (1988c) studied 695 athletes in 15 sports and noted that 1.6% of male college athletes and 4.2% of female college athletes satisfied criteria for anorexia nervosa outlined in the *Diagnostic and Statistical Manual of Mental Disorders III-Revised (DSM III-R)* (American Psychiatric Association, 1987). Also, 14.3% of male athletes and 39.2% of female athletes met the criteria for bulimia nervosa. Research on college women in general indicates that bulimia nervosa may be present in 1–5% of young women and less than 1% of young men when the more restrictive criteria of *DSM III-R* are used (Johnson, Lewis, Love, Stuckey, & Lewis, 1983; Pope, Hudson, Yurgelun-Todd, & Hudson, 1984; Pyle, Halvorson,

Neuman, & Mitchell, 1986). The prevalence rate of anorexia nervosa among adolescent women is approximately .01% to .00125% (*DSM III-R*) and among young men is considerably less. Based on the findings of Burckes-Miller and Black (1988c), it seems that eating disorder tendencies are more prevalent among athletes than the college population in general. Ballet dancers also are said to have a rate of anorexia nervosa 10 times that of the general population (Garner & Garfinkel, 1980). In addition, eating disorders have been referred to as an occupational hazard of models, dancers, gymnasts, figure skaters, runners, swimmers, wrestlers, jockeys, and fitness instructors (Moriarty & Moriarty, 1988).

Media

The current focus of the media reflects the cultural emphasis on physical fitness and leanness. Athletes may be especially susceptible because they often model and epitomize the athletic or fitness look that is accentuated by the media. In addition, thinness is also equated in the media with sex appeal, popularity, status, self-esteem, happiness, control, achievement, and enhanced quality of life.

Athletes may also experience pressures to be thin that are designed to influence the general population. Popular women's magazines publicize diet articles and advertisements for *light, fat free* products; movies carry the same message indicating that thin is chic; and television carries the message, day in and day out, that one can only be loved and respected if slim (Connelly & Black, 1989; Garner et al., 1980; Silverstein & Perdue, 1986).

The media may also influence the degree of body satisfaction among both the general population and athletes. In a *Glamour* magazine survey of 33,000 women, 75% of the respondents reported feeling too fat, although according to height/weight charts, only 25% were overweight ("Feeling fat," 1984). It is well publicized that over 80% of girls, before age 13, have been on a weight loss diet, in contrast to 10% of the boys (Hawkins, Turell, & Jason, 1983). In a more recent study, however, it has been noted that 63% of the 675 high school girls were dieting, although on average these girls were 5% below normal weight. Among the 660 boys in this study, 17% were dieting and on average were 17.5% below normal weight (Leichner & Gertler, 1989). In a study of athletes, Burckes-Miller and Black (1988a) found that approximately one-seventh of the athletes thought they were fat even though they had lost weight and were not overweight.

Roles of Men and Women

In this day of rapidly changing sex roles, both men and women are encountering new stressors. Athletes may experience role conflict and be faced with the dilemma of whether to behave according to what is expected of them in their ascribed sex role or whether to behave as an *athlete* (McPherson, 1982). It has been shown that the mesomorphic male silhouette is associated with perceived masculinity (Striegel-Moore et al., 1986). The male athlete, then, is expected to look muscular as well as be successful. Men today also feel the stress of being involved in fitness activities as well as with their families and friends. There is an expectation in the roles of both men and women to be successful at a career and to be in good physical condition too.

Female athletes may be placed at greater risk for psychological stress in general (Striegel-Moore et al., 1986). For example, women have many more choices related to both family life and careers, and they experience contradictory pressures to be sophisticated and successful, yet fashionable and thin.

Community

College campuses are stressful and semiclosed communities that may intensify the sociocultural pressures to be thin (Striegel-Moore et al., 1986). College athletes are also a part of many other semiclosed environments on campus such as the dormitory, fraternity or sorority, student organizations, etc. Perhaps coupled with an increase in role responsibilities and added academic stresses, these conditions separately or in combination may exacerbate the likelihood of maladaptive eating and exercise attitudes and behaviors and the use of unhealthy weight loss methods among college athletes (Black & Burckes-Miller, 1988; Burckes-Miller & Black, 1988a).

According to Crago, Yates, Beutler, and Arizmendi (1985), pathology typically begins after a person has entered the athletic subculture. In addition, the occurrence of eating pathology in athletics seems to be linked to an emphasis on weight and appearance as opposed to the stressful nature of training and competition (Garner & Garfinkel, 1980). Exercise or physical activity in and of itself, however, may not precipitate eating disorders but if fitness/sport programs are presented with an emphasis on body shape, they may well serve as a precipitator for individuals predisposed to an eating disorder (Moriarty & Moriarty, 1988).

The type of sport or level of competition, however, may also make a difference in possibly predisposing an athlete to an eating disorder. Borgen and Corbin (1987) showed that individuals engaging in body-focused activities or lean-emphasizing sports were preoccupied with food and weight and had a tendency toward an eating disorder. Running is often a sport of choice for those with eating disorders. Isolation, self-regimentation, and self-deprivation, all which may increase the likelihood of eating disorders, are socially acceptable for runners. Katz (1986) suggested that extreme exercise can serve to trigger anorexia nervosa in persons already at risk. In addition, he noted that with runners, other forces are often set into motion such as a truly diminished appetite, increased narcissistic investment in the body, and elevated production of endorphins.

Peers

The influence of peers may be very important to athletes, especially with an emphasis on teamwork and team participation. The use of strategies to regulate weight or food intake may be a way to gain acceptance and feel included by one's peers in athletics. In some sports where there is pressure to maintain low body weight, peer pressure may be extreme as evidenced by the seemingly high prevalence of eating disorders among athletes in sports such as running, dance, and wrestling (Burckes-Miller & Black, 1988c; Moriarty & Moriarty, 1988). In addition, athletes may teach each other unhealthy ways to manage weight or food consumption. Thompson and Schwartz (1982) noted that half of the women who reported vomiting knew another woman who vomited and many had been taught by them. There may be a contagious effect with eating disordered methods spreading among team members especially when less successful athletes prone to eating disorders observe more successful athletes who use unhealthy weight control methods. There may be a sense of comradery, and eating disorder behaviors may gain group acceptance.

Little is known about the impact of peer pressure specifically as it relates to athletes. It seems reasonable, however, that athletes would learn from fellow athletes about unhealthy weight control methods in the same way they learn from each other about aspects of their training such as techniques for skill acquisition, posturing, etc.

Coaches and Other Authority Figures

Coaches may play a key role in the physical, psychological, and social development of young athletes. Some coaches are genuinely concerned about the athlete's welfare, while others may be more concerned about winning than the athlete's physical and mental well-being. The U.S. Olympic Committee (1987) has raised several interesting points, one of which is that all coaches are in a position to have a profound influence on young, impressionable athletes, especially in the area of weight control. Some practices of coaches may serve to encourage eating disordered attitudes and behavior. For example, group or public weigh-ins as well as posting of percentage body fat may overemphasize low body weight. Many coaches have upper weight limits for athletes on their teams but not lower limits. The message given to young athletes may be that low body weight is desirable and necessary for success. In addition, coaches' verbal statements may reinforce the necessity of unhealthy lower body weight. An innocent remark about an athlete being out of shape or overweight may lead to drastic actions by the athlete to prove otherwise. Comments that create an implied expectation with no guidance about how to proceed in a safe and effective manner may be harmful regardless of intent.

Coaches may not have an incentive to attend to anomalies in weight and eating habits. Moore indicated that the coach's success is contingent upon the athlete's performance (Zucker et al., 1985). It is known that a coach's reputation is built on the ability to develop elite athletes. In addition, the competitive advantage may be lost for athletic scholarships due to excessive weight. Also, there may be concern among coaches that if an athlete enrolls in therapy for an eating disorder, that person may not be inclined to compete and participate in sport.

Family

The family may affect an athlete's susceptibility to an eating disorder in several ways. First, families may subtly sanction unhealthy behaviors and attitudes and the use of pathogenic weight loss methods. Second, family members may encourage athletes to be competitive and to succeed at their sport. Third, to gain family approval and recognition, young athletes may feel compelled to use pathogenic weight loss methods in order to achieve. Finally, an athlete is also at risk for developing an eating disorder if someone in the family specifically reinforces efforts to lose weight (Striegel-Moore et al., 1986).

Family characteristics may predispose some athletes to an eating disorder. Strober, Salkin, Burroughs, and Marrell (1982) found a four-fold greater rate of alcoholism in the first-degree relatives of bulimic-anorexics than in relatives of (caloric) restricting anorexics (16% vs.

4%, $p < .02$). Unipolar depression has been shown to occur two to four times more frequently in first-degree relatives of both anorexic and bulimic patients than in the general population (Hudson, Pope, Jonas, & Yurgelan-Todd, 1983; Strober et al., 1982). Studies have also shown the proportion of patients with positive family histories for eating disorders ranges from 4% to 7% (Hall, 1978; Hudson et al., 1983). Kalucy, Crisp, and Harding (1977) reported peculiar dietary habits and anorexia or severe weight phobia in 27% of the mothers and 16% of the fathers in the 56 cases studied. In addition, Minuchin, Rosman, and Baker (1978) identified five primary personality characteristics of the family that are fairly common in anorexic families. They are enmeshment, overprotectiveness, rigidity, conflict avoidance, and poor conflict resolution skills.

Conclusions

This paper points out the major impact of the environment on athletes' susceptibility to eating disorders. The intent is to provide a context in order to account for the seemingly disproportionate number of athletes who satisfy criteria for eating disorders, exhibit eating disorder characteristics, and utilize unhealthy weight loss methods. The athlete's environment as a major contributing factor would not be surprising according to Learning Theory. Learning Theory presumes that a person's environment contributes to the formation of habits and serves to maintain lifestyles (cf. Bandura, 1977). Several environmental factors are presented that seem to influence the occurrence and maintenance of unhealthy attitudes and behaviors and eating disorders among athletes. The factors considered were culture, media, roles of men and women, peers, coaches and other authority figures, and family. These factors were meant to be representative, but not exhaustive.

When the environment of the athlete is examined, there are a number of important, but as yet, unanswered questions. The foremost question is whether there is *truly* a higher incidence of eating disorders among athletes. It also seems prudent to clarify whether athletic performance exacerbates preexistent inclinations and encourages the initiation of unhealthy methods of managing body weight and food consumption or whether athletics mediates or prevents an eating disorder. Another question is to determine if eating disorder behaviors are functional and short-term or pathological and more difficult to abate. Related to these concerns are what type of sociological factors are dominant and account for the greatest percentage of variance collectively or have the most profound affect individually. Future research might examine the specific environmental demands of particular sports to determine the relationship between specific demands and eating pathology among athletes.

The answers to these and other questions are vital, but until data are available, interventions that focus on the environment and lifestyles need to be a primary focus. Athletes currently seem vulnerable and appear to function in an environment which perpetuates unhealthy attitudes and behaviors as well as pathogenic weight control methods. Interventions need to be approached from a perspective of changing both the athlete's environment and the athlete's own perceptions and behaviors in relationship to the environment. The concentration in both instances needs to be less on sport and more on health.

For example, the media might focus on healthy ways to control weight through proper nutrition (e.g., Hand, 1989a, 1989b). Coaches and perhaps family members might stress healthful ways of competing instead of promoting the attitude that *winning* brings total fulfillment and completeness. Another possibility is to identify the demands placed on athletes by society, the community, peers, coaches, and family. Knowledge of these circumstances could lead to appropriate actions to ameliorate unfavorable conditions that may be precipitating factors for eating disorders. These examples are provided to suggest that if the environment and the athlete's response to it could be modified, the prevalence of anorexia nervosa and bulimia nervosa might be dramatically affected.

In summary, this paper has focused on interplay among the environmental factors as a way to explain the apparent increase of eating disorders among athletes. Social and cultural influences do not necessarily cause eating disorders. Society is mediated by the individual as well as inherited characteristics that may be either predisposing or protecting factors in the development of an eating disorder (Garner, Garfinkel, & Olmsted, 1983). The characteristics of an athlete's involvement in sports are often determined by the social structure of the environment in which the social action occurs (McPherson, 1982). Thus, in order to assist athletes in healthy sport competition, it seems imperative to understand the athlete's whole environment as well as the impact of body weight regulation and attitudes and behaviors toward dietary intake and physical activity. Then the Duchess's statement might be modified as follows, "One can never be too *healthy* or too rich."

References

American Psychiatric Association. (1987). *Diagnostic and statistical manual of mental disorders* (3rd ed., revised). Washington, DC: Author.

Bandura, A. (1977). Self-efficacy: Toward a unifying theory of behavior change. *Psychological Review, 84,* 191–215.

Black, D. R., & Burckes-Miller, M. E. (1988). Male and female college athletes: Use of anorexia nervosa and bulimia nervosa weight loss methods. *Research Quarterly for Exercise and Sport, 59,* 252–256.

Borgen, J. S., & Corbin, C. B. (1987). Eating disorders among female athletes. *The Physician and Sportsmedicine, 15*(2), 88–95.

Brumberg, J. J. (1988). *Fasting girls: The emergence of anorexia nervosa as a modern disease.* Cambridge: Harvard University Press.

Burckes-Miller, M. E., & Black, D. R. (1988a). Behaviors and attitudes associated with eating disorders: Perceptions of college athletes about food and weight. *Health Education Research, Theory and Practice, 3,* 203–208.

Burckes-Miller, M. E., & Black, D. R. (1988b). Eating disorders: A problem in athletics? *Health Education, 19*(1), 22–25.

Burckes-Miller, M. E., & Black, D. R. (1988c). Male and female college athletes: Prevalence of anorexia nervosa and bulimia nervosa. *Athletic Training, 23,* 137–140.

Connelly, K., & Black, D. R. (1989). *Sex differences in media promotion of a thin body standard: Further considerations.* Manuscript submitted for publication.

Crago, M., Yates, A., Beutler, L. E., & Arizmendi, T. G. (1985). Height-weight ratios among female athletes: Are collegiate athletics the precursor to an anorexic syndrome. *International Journal of Eating Disorders, 4,* 79–87.

Feeling fat in a thin society. (1984). *Glamour, 82,* pp. 161–164.

Garner, D. M., & Garfinkel, P. (1980). Socio-cultural factors in the development of anorexia nervosa. *Psychological Medicine, 10,* 646–657.

Garner, D. M., Garfinkel, P. E., & Olmsted, M. P. (1983). An overview of sociocultural factors in the development of anorexia nervosa. In P. L. Darby et al. (Eds.), *Anorexia nervosa: Recent development in research* (pp. 65–82). New York: Alan R. Liss.

Garner, D. M., Garfinkel, P. E., Schwartz, D., & Thompson, M. (1980). Cultural expectations of thinness in women. *Psychological Reports, 47,* 483–491.

Hall, A. (1978). Family structure and relationships of 50 female anorexia nervosa patients. *Australian and New Zealand Journal of Psychiatry, 12,* 263–268.

Hand, C. (Producer). (1989a). *Afraid to eat: Eating disorders and student athletes.* (Videotape). Wilkes-Barre, PA: Karol Media.

Hand, C. (Producer). (1989b). *Out of balance: Nutrition and weight.* (Videotape). Wilkes-Barre, PA: Karol Media.

Hawkins, R. C., Turell, S., & Jason, L. J. (1983). Desirable and undesirable masculine and feminine traits in relation to students' dietary tendencies and body image dissatisfaction. *Sex Roles, 9*, 705–724.

Hudson, J. I., Pope, H. G., Jonas, J. M., & Yurgelun-Todd, D. (1983). A family study of anorexia nervosa and bulimia. *British Journal of Psychiatry, 142*, 133–138.

Johnson, C. L., Lewis, G., Love, S., Stuckey, M., & Lewis, L. (1983). A descriptive survey of dieting and bulimic behavior in a female high school population. In D. E. Redfern (Ed.), *Understanding anorexia nervosa and bulimia: Report from the Fourth Ross Conference on Medical Research* (pp. 14–18). Columbus, OH: Ross Laboratories.

Kalucy, R. S., Crisp, A. H., & Harding, B. (1977). A study of 56 families with anorexia nervosa. *British Journal of Medical Psychology, 50*, 381–395.

Kaplan, A. S., & Woodside, D. B. (1987). Biological aspects of anorexia nervosa and bulimia nervosa. *Journal of Consulting and Clinical Psychology, 55*, 645–653.

Katz, J. L. (1986). Long distance running, anorexia nervosa, and bulimia: Report of two cases. *Comprehensive Psychiatry, 27*, 74–78.

Leichner, P., & Gertler, A. (1989). Prevalence and incidence studies of anorexia nervosa. In B. J. Blinder, B. F. Chaitin, R. Goldstein (Eds.), *The eating disorders* (pp. 131–149). Great Neck, NY: PMA Publishing Corp.

Mallick, M. J., Whipple, T. W., & Huerta, E. (1987). Behavioral and psychological traits of weight conscious teenagers: A comparison of eating disordered patients and high and low risk groups. *Adolescence, 22*, 157–185.

Mazur, A. (1986). U.S. trends in feminine beauty and overadaptation. *The Journal of Sex Research, 22*, 281–303.

McArthur, J. W., Bullen, B. A., Beitius, I. Z., Pagano, M., Badger, T. M., & Klibanski, A. (1980). Hypothalamic amenorrhea in runners of normal body composition. *Endocrinology Research Communications, 7*, 13–25.

McPherson, B. (1982). The child in competitive sport: Influence of social milieu. In R. Magill, M. Ash, & F. Smoll (Eds.), *Children in sport* (chap. 18, pp. 247–268). Champaign, IL: Human Kinetics.

Minuchin, S., Rosman, B. L., & Baker, L. (1978). *Psychosomatic families: Anorexia nervosa in context.* Cambridge, MA: Harvard University Press.

Mitchell, J. E., & Eckert, E. D. (1987). Scope and significance of eating disorders. *Journal of Consulting and Clinical Psychology, 55*, 628–634.

Moriarty, D., & Moriarty, M. (1988). *Socio-cultural influences in eating disorders: Focus on sport/fitness programs.* Unpublished manuscript.

Olmsted, M. P., & Garner, D. M. (1984). The significance of self-induced vomiting as a weight control method among college women. Unpublished manuscript.

Pope, H. G., Jr., Hudson, J. I., Yurgelun-Todd, D., & Hudson, M. S. (1984). Prevalence of anorexia nervosa and bulimia in three student populations. *International Journal of Eating Disorders, 3*, 45–51.

Pyle, R. L., Halvorson, P. A., Neuman, P. A., & Mitchell, J. E. (1986). The increasing prevalence of bulimia in freshman college students. *International Journal of Eating Disorders, 5,* 631–647.

Rosen, L., McKeag, D., Hough, D., & Curley, V. (1986). Pathogenic weight control behavior in female athletes. *The Physician and Sportsmedicine, 14,* 79–86.

Rosenzweig, M., & Spruill, J. (1987). Twenty years after Twiggy: A retrospective investigation of bulimic-like behaviors. *International Journal of Eating Disorders, 6,* 59–65.

Shephard, R. (1986). *Fitness of a nation: Lessons from the Canada Fitness Survey* (pp. 4–15). New York: Karger.

Silverstein, B., & Perdue, L. (1986). The role of the mass media in promoting a thin standard of bodily attractiveness for women. *Sex Roles, 14,* 519–532.

Silverstein, B., Perdue, L., Peterson, B., Vogel, L., & Fantini D. (1986). Possible causes of the thin standard of bodily attractiveness for women. *International Journal of Eating Disorders, 5,* 907–916.

Striegel-Moore, R. H., Silberstein, L. R., & Rodin, J. (1986). Toward an understanding of risk factors for bulimia. *American Psychologist, 41,* 246–263.

Strober, M., & Humphrey, L. L. (1987). Familial contributions to the etiology and course of anorexia nervosa and bulimia. *Journal of Consulting and Clinical Psychology, 55,* 654–659.

Strober, M., Salkin, B., Burroughs, J., & Marrell, W. (1982). Validity of the bulimia-restrictor distinction in anorexia nervosa: Parental personality characteristics and family psychiatry morbidity. *Journal of Nervous and Mental Diseases, 170,* 345–351.

Thompson, M. G., & Schwartz, D. M. (1982). Life adjustment of women with anorexia nervosa and anorexia-like behavior. *International Journal of Eating Disorders, 1,* 47–60.

U.S. Olympic Committee. (1987). *Sports nutrition: Eating disorders.* Omaha, NE: Swanson Center for Nutrition, University of Nebraska Medical Center.

Wooley, S. C., & Wooley, O. W. (1981). Overeating as a substance abuse. In N. Mello (Ed.), *Advances in substance abuse* (Vol. 2). Greenwich, CT: JAI.

Zucker, P., Avener, J., Bayder, S., Brotman, A., Moore, K., & Zimmerman, J. (1985). Eating disorders in young athletes. *The Physician and Sportsmedicine, 13*(11), 88–106.

Author Notes

The authors wish to thank the following individuals for reviewing an earlier draft of this manuscript and for their helpful comments and suggestions: Jennifer D. Boynton, Jane M. Clary, Martha A. Dunbar,

Barbara B. Jones, Rhonda I. Musikar, and Della M. Schaffhauser. The authors are also indebted to three anonymous reviewers for their feedback and recommendations about how to enhance the manuscript.

Preparation of this article was supported in part by funds provided to David R. Black from the American Alliance for Health, Physical Education, Recreation and Dance and the Association for the Advancement of Health Education.

3

Eating Disorders and Athletes: Current Issues and Future Research

DAVID R. BLACK
SUZANNE E. HELD

This chapter identifies current issues related to eating disorders and athletes and lists questions for future research. Seven issues are identified from a review of books and articles. The issues relate to the following: (a) prevalence and measurement, (b) focus of intervention, (c) origin of the problem, (d) sport versus individual, (e) gender, (f) duration of the problem, and (g) cause of the problem. Research questions based on each of the issues are presented. The issues and research questions addressed are designed to promote critical thinking, to further challenge underlying assumptions, and to encourage future investigations.

This chapter was written specifically to formalize new issues related to eating disorders and athletes and to consolidate ones identified previously. The issues are discussed to note important underlying assumptions and to encourage critical thinking pertaining to research and practice. The issues also provide perspective about the severity, urgency, and necessity of clinical intervention.

Seven issues related to eating disorders and athletes are explored; they are presented as questions: (a) What are the problems in determining the actual prevalence and measurement of eating disorders among athletes? *(prevalence and measurement);* (b) Who should be the focus of intervention, those diagnosed with an eating disorder or those with pathogenic behaviors and attitudes and who use unhealthy weight loss methods? *(focus of intervention);* (c) Are eating disorders initiated by athletics or are people with eating disorders attracted to athletics? *(origin of the problem);* (d) Is the problem sport related or specific to individuals? *(sport vs. individual);* (e) Are eating disorders gender specific? *(gender);* (f) Is the problem prevalent only during athletic involvement/participation or does it continue after formal involvement in sport ends? *(duration of the problem);* and (g) Who is the cause of the problem? *(cause of the problem).* These questions are presented discretely, but in reality may overlap.

The questions were generated from a review of books and articles identified through a computer literature search. The search was restricted to materials published in the last decade. Older publications were also identified from reference lists of more recently published articles. In addition, hand searches were completed of key journals such as the *International Journal of Eating Disorders* and *The Physician and Sportsmedicine.* Even though approximately 70 articles primarily related to eating disorders and athletes were reviewed, the search was not intended to be exhaustive. The issues and research questions presented below are based on the works included in the bibliography at the end of this chapter. Consequently, the majority of statements do not include citations because this would be too cumbersome. When references are cited, they refer to specific information, examples, theories, and procedures. (These specific citations are included in the Bibliography along with all the articles reviewed.) Each issue is discussed below and future research questions are presented in a separate section and table.

Prevalence and Measurement

The primary question related to prevalence and measurement is what is the actual number of athletes with an eating disorder. Several concerns become imminent when this question is addressed. The concerns include how to identify the existence of an eating disorder, and whether diagnosis or associated behaviors, attitudes, and weight loss methods should be the predominant focus of intervention.

Many different assessments and criteria have been reported in the research literature. For example, the Eating Disorders Inventory (EDI) was used by Borgen and Corbin (1987), and the Eating Attitudes Test (EAT) was used by Szmukler, Eisler, Gollies, and Hayward (1985) and Garner and Garfinkel (1980). The most current and widely accepted method of assessment is the *Diagnostic and Statistical Manual of Mental Disorders (DSM-III-R)* (American Psychiatric Association, 1987a). Its criteria for anorexia nervosa and bulimia nervosa are presented in Table 3.1. These criteria are used by the medical and psychological communities for diagnosis and decisions about treatment. It is important for investigators of athletes to be aware of changes in diagnostic criteria and to incorporate these revisions into their research protocols. Review of past literature pertaining to athletes indicates that one of the reasons prevalence rates differ among studies may be due to the measurement criteria or to different assessment methods used by various investigators.

Variance in prevalance rates may also be due to the nature of self-report data. Data collected via surveys need to be verified. One method of verification is to conduct structured interviews designed specifically to elicit confirmatory information (Fairburn, 1984). Another factor that may be considered is who collects the information. If a coach familiar

Table 3.1

Two Eating Disorders from the Diagnostic and Statistical Manual of Mental Disorders

Diagnostic Criteria

307.10 Anorexia Nervosa

A. Refusal to maintain body weight over a minimal normal weight for age and height, e.g., weight loss leading to maintenance of body weight 15% below that expected.

B. Intense fear of gaining weight or becoming fat, even though underweight.

C. Disturbance in the way in which one's body weight, size, or shape is experienced, e.g., the person claims to "feel fat" even when emaciated, believes that one area of the body is "too fat" even when obviously underweight.

D. In females, absence of at least three consecutive menstrual cycles when otherwise expected to occur (primary or secondary amenorrhea). (A woman is considered to have amenorrhea if her periods occur only following hormone administration, e.g., estrogen.)

307.51 Bulimia Nervosa

A. Recurrent episodes of binge eating (rapid consumption of a large amount of food in a discrete period of time).

B. A feeling of lack of control over eating behavior during the eating binges.

C. The person regularly engages in either self-induced vomiting, use of laxatives or diuretics, strict dieting or fasting, or vigorous exercise in order to prevent weight gain.

D. A minimum average of two binge eating episodes a week for at least three months.

E. Persistent overconcern with body shape and weight.

with the athlete or sports program administers surveys or conducts interviews, the athlete may be reluctant to provide candid and valid information. Consequently, prevalence rates may be even higher and the problem greater than reported in studies where coaches administered surveys.

Focus of Intervention

The issue addressing who should be the focus of intervention, those considered eating disordered or those demonstrating pathogenic or eating disorder symptoms, can be put into perspective by using theory as well as clinical diagnostic criteria. In terms of clinical diagnostic criteria, the focus in the past has been *disease/disorder oriented* and on the number of athletes who might be considered anorexic or bulimic. There has been less emphasis on individuals with pathogenic or eating disorder symptoms. If there is a desire to remain disease/disorder oriented and to focus more on symptoms of eating disorders and pathogenic behaviors, the use of another *DSM-III-R* diagnosis, "Eating Disorders Not Otherwise Specified (#307.50)," might be considered. Examples of eating disorders not otherwise specified from the *Quick Reference to the Diagnostic Criteria from DSM-III-R* (American Psychiatric Association, 1987b) include the following: "(a) a person of average weight who does not have binge eating episodes, but frequently engages in self-induced vomiting for fear of gaining weight, (b) all of the features of anorexia nervosa in a female except absence of menses, and (c) all of the features of bulimia nervosa except the frequency of binge eating episodes" (p. 65).

A recent theoretical article by Hyner, Melby, Petosa, Seehafer, and Black (1988) also may help clarify this issue. The authors indicate that the bulk of medical services used and medical costs incurred are the result of a small percentage of people who are frequent users of the medical system. Conversely, subjects who engage in unhealthy behaviors but have opportunities to prevent major medical problems are often overlooked. Perhaps the probability for success is more realistic for individuals with few long-standing behavioral and/or physiological risk factors than for those diagnosed as diseased and who incur the bulk of the medical costs. In the eating disorders area, it has been established that treatments for those diagnosed as diseased are generally ineffective, and recidivism rates are dismal (Agras & Kraemer, 1984; Fairburn, 1984).

The point is that there are far more athletes who engage in behaviors and attitudes and use weight loss methods that are unhealthy than there are athletes who are eating disordered. That is not to say that those with eating disorders are not important or that they should not receive treatment or services. Promoting positive behaviors and attitudes related to food, exercise, and weight loss may, however, promote health and prevent major medical sequelae.

Origin of the Problem

Another issue addresses the origin of eating disorders in athletes— whether eating disorders are initiated by participation in sport or whether people with eating disorders are attracted to athletics. One way to approach this issue is from a theoretical perspective. Burckes-Miller and Black (see Chapter 2) present the thesis that the etiology of eating disorders among athletes is related primarily, but not exclusively, to sociocultural factors. The sociocultural factors introduced by the authors include culture, media, roles of men and women, peers, coaches and other authority figures, and family. These factors may explain both sides of the origin issue. For example, during participation in athletics, pressure from peers and teammates may lead to athletes using unhealthy weight management techniques. Prior to athletic participation, a person may be influenced by what culture and media depict as the ideal look of being thin, muscular, and healthy. Consequently, a person may become involved in athletics to achieve the thin, muscular look.

Sport Versus Individual

This issue asks whether the problem is sport related or specific to the individual. There are several ways the occurrence of eating disorders may be related to a specific sport. Many sports require that certain weights be maintained in order to participate. For example, wrestlers often are asked to lower their weight to the next class and those not making their weight classification forfeit their team position for the match. In other sports, low body fat is encouraged. For instance, cross country runners who carry less body fat are presumed to be more efficient in competition. Hence, weight loss may be encouraged as a means of obtaining a competitive edge. Finally, the aesthetic appeal of a lean figure is crucial in some sports to obtain the scores needed to win in competition. Distance running, gymnastics, figure skating, diving, synchronized swimming, and ballet are among the sports where a low body weight may bestow a competitive advantage or may be important for appearance (Brownell, Steen, & Wilmore, 1987).

A particular sport, however, may not be the issue. The problem may be the individual. A person may become involved in a particular sport as an acceptable way to achieve and maintain a weight that is desirable to them. Competitive athletics provides the eating disordered person a socially acceptable context to exercise excessively, set low weight goals, and practice eating disordered attitudes and behaviors. Another reason an athlete may engage in harmful behaviors is for peer approval and acceptance. Engaging in a similar socially unacceptable behavior may be a means to *bond* with another individual or be included in a particular athletic group.

Gender

An important issue is whether eating disorders are related to a specific sex. While it is true that women more often than men present with eating disorders, men should not be overlooked. Many past studies only focus on women and women in sport (e.g., Borgen & Corbin, 1987; Falls & Humphrey, 1978; Garner & Garfinkel, 1980; Overdorf, 1987). The current prevalence ratio of eating disorders of 10–20 women to 1 man may be, at least in part, a function of the lack of measurement rather than valid differences.

It also seems suspect that only women athletes are affected. There are obvious differences between men and women, but both sexes are influenced by remarks and expectations of others. Statements such as "Your performance would improve with weight loss" may result in athletes using harmful weight loss methods to obtain performance goals. Both men and women participate in sports emphasizing leanness (e.g., gymnastics and dance). Men, however, may have a disadvantage not experienced by women. Paradoxically, men are expected to be both bulky and muscular, yet trim. Media further emphasizes this by portraying a strong, muscular man as a hero. Not all humans are the perfect ectomorph or mesomorph and many may practice eating disordered techniques to try and achieve this societal *ideal*.

Duration of the Problem

The issue of duration addresses whether the problem is prevalent only during formal athletics. Duration can be divided into three time intervals. These intervals suggest the following temporal possibilities regarding eating disorders in athletics: (a) short-term or functional and only occur during the season but not the off-season, (b) full-term and happen during the athletic season and during the off-season, or (c) long-term and transpire during athletic participation and after formal athletics ends. Combinations of the three time intervals are also possibilities. For example, an athlete may exhibit an eating disorder only during the competitive season, but once formal involvement in athletics is terminated, the person may continue the eating disorder.

Each possibility may have implications for permanency and severity of the eating disorder. Several reinforcement principles from psychology and Learning Theory may apply. First, the more often behaviors occur, the more difficult they are to break. Second, the greater the perceived benefits of the behaviors (e.g., performing well, winning a competition, or achieving the aesthetic ideal), the more difficult the behaviors are to eliminate.

Cause of the Problem

A final issue is who to blame for the problem. The research literature is full of ideas about who is at fault for the problem of eating disorders among athletes. Coaches, trainers, and their staff, but primarily coaches, have been the main people identified as culprits. This may or may not be accurate. A review of Chapter 2 by Burckes-Miller and Black suggests that there may be several sociocultural factors, in addition to coaches, that contribute to an athlete's eating disorder. All of these factors, cumulatively or some in particular, may have a significant influence on the development and maintenance of an eating disorder.

If coaches do have a significant impact, as some literature suggests (e.g., Benson, 1990; Chopak & Taylor-Nicholson, 1990), then it seems prudent to examine factors that influence coaches. The examination of these influences may lead to opportunities to institute changes and to affect the occurrence of eating disorders among athletes. Figure 3.1 presents several possible factors that may impact coaches. The figure indicates that coaches do not operate independently and are influenced by a variety of factors. These factors, in turn, may affect the advice they provide to athletes.

Research Questions

The ideas presented in this paper about issues related to eating disorders and athletes will, hopefully, be useful to those connected with athletics and will engender future research. Studies are needed to exam-

Figure 3.1.   Sociocultural influences on coaches.

ine and further clarify each of the issues presented in this paper. Table 3.2 lists research questions based on each of the issues.

Summary

The issues and research questions selected are germane to athletes and eating disorders. The intent of this chapter has been to encourage the consideration of a multitude of issues and to present relevant research questions. Hopefully, this chapter clarifies the main issues and will lead to further challenges of underlying assumptions and to critical thinking. The area of eating disorders and athletes is in its infancy. Research opportunities are abundant and many key questions remain to be investigated. Theory should guide research and novel research projects will help to clarify current issues and add to knowledge in this area.

Table 3.2

Research Questions Pertaining to Current Issues Related to Eating Disorders and Athletes

Prevalence and Measurement

What diagnostic criteria should be used for eating disorders among athletes?

What information should be included in a questionnaire about athletes and eating disorders?

What is the best assessment measure for diagnosing an eating disorder among athletes and those who may be *at risk* for developing an eating disorder?

How valid and reliable are self-report data from athletes and how can validity and reliability be improved?

Does interviewing athletes elicit more accurate information and who is the best person to conduct the interview?

Focus of Intervention

When is the appropriate time to intervene with an athlete who is eating disordered or exhibiting unhealthy behaviors and attitudes related to food, exercise, and weight?

When do pathogenic attitudes and behaviors and the use of unhealthy weight loss methods by athletes become a concern or lead to an eating disorder?

Can eating disorders be prevented through early education and counseling?

What information prevents eating disorders among athletes?

At what educational level (e.g., elementary, junior high, secondary, etc.) should athletes be informed about eating disorders?

What is the best way to modify the behavior and attitudes of an athlete related to an eating disorder?

Will an athlete with an eating disorder who receives counseling terminate participation in athletics?

Origin of the Problem

What are the reasons athletes participate in sport? Do these reasons change over time?

Is there a type of athlete who is predisposed to an eating disorder?

Do athletes respond differently than others to sociological influences related to eating disorders?

What changes in athletics would promote healthy weight-related behaviors and attitudes?

What role models and cultural figures could positively influence athletes and help prevent and abate eating disorders?

Continued on next page

Sport Versus Individual

Are athletes from specific sports more at risk to develop an eating disorder or is a given type of person more likely to become eating disordered?

Do certain weight-related behaviors and attitudes occur more among athletes in particular sports?

What motivates an athlete to choose a sport that emphasizes leanness or low body weight?

What are the physiological and psychological risks versus the competitive advantages of low body weight for young athletes?

Is there a *safe* weight level that serves as a performance advantage but does not compromise short- or long-term health?

How do athletic peers influence each others' weight-related attitudes and behaviors and use of unhealthy weight loss methods?

Gender

What are the differences between female and male athletes and the prevalence of eating disorders and pathogenic attitudes and behavior?

Do men and women respond differently to weight demands of sport?

Do men and women differ in the reasons they participate in sport and reasons they lose weight?

Do men and women choose sports emphasizing leanness for different reasons?

Duration of the Problem

How does the duration of an eating disorder of an athlete affect the severity of the disorder?

How does the duration of athletic participation affect the occurrence and severity of an eating disorder?

Do short-term or functional eating disorders lead to long-term disorders among athletes?

Do former athletes with unhealthy weight-related attitudes and behaviors develop eating disorders?

Cause of the Problem

Who is best suited (e.g., coach, health educator, etc.) to give advice and information to athletes?

What knowledge is necessary for coaching personnel regarding eating disorders, nutrition, and weight management?

How often should the coaching staff conduct weigh-ins of athletes?

What behaviors and attitudes need to be encouraged by parents and athletic personnel in order to prevent and abate eating disorders among athletes?

Do former eating disordered athletes negatively influence others involved in athletics?

Bibliography

Agras, W. S., & Kraemer, H. C. (1984). The treatment of anorexia nervosa: Do different treatments have different outcomes? In A. J. Stunkard & E. Stellar (Eds.), *Eating and its disorders* (pp. 193–207). New York: Raven.

American Psychiatric Association. (1980). *Diagnostic and statistical manual of mental disorders* (3rd ed.). Washington, DC: Author.

American Psychiatric Association. (1987a). *Diagnostic and statistical manual of mental disorders* (3rd ed., revised). Washington, DC: Author.

American Psychiatric Association. (1987b). *Quick reference to the diagnostic criteria from DSM-III-R*. Washington, DC: Author.

Benson, J., Gillien, D. M., Bourdet, K., & Loosli, A. R. (1985). Inadequate nutrition and chronic calorie restriction in adolescent ballerinas. *The Physician and Sportsmedicine, 13*(10), 79–90.

Benson, R. (1991). Weight control among elite women swimmers. In D. R. Black (Ed.), *Eating disorders among athletes: Theory, issues, and research* (pp. 97–110). Reston, VA: American Alliance for Health, Physical Education, Recreation and Dance.

Black, D. R., & Burckes-Miller, M. E. (1988). Male and female college athletes: Use of anorexia nervosa and bulimia nervosa weight loss methods. *Research Quarterly for Exercise and Sport, 59*, 252–256.

Blumenthal, J. A., O'Toole, L. C., & Chang, J. L. (1984). Is running an analogue of anorexia nervosa? An empirical study of obligatory running and anorexia nervosa. *JAMA, 252*, 520–523.

Blumenthal, J. A., Rose, S., & Chang, J. L. (1985). Anorexia nervosa and exercise: Implications from recent findings. *Sports Medicine, 2*, 237–247.

Boe, E. E. (1985). The physiological and psychological consequences of excessive weight loss in athletics. *Athletic Training, 20*, 238–242.

Borgen, J. S., & Corbin, C. B. (1987). Eating disorders among female athletes, *The Physician and Sportsmedicine, 15*(2), 88–95.

Brooks-Gunn, J., Warren, M. P., & Hamilton, L. H. (1986). The relationship of eating problems and amenorrhea in ballet dancers. *Medicine and Science in Sports and Exercise, 19*, 41–44.

Brownell, K. D., Steen, S. N., & Wilmore, J. H. (1987). Weight regulation practices in athletes: Analysis of metabolic and health effects. *Medicine and Science in Sports and Exercise, 19*, 546–556.

Buickel, S. (1983). Anorexia nervosa and bulimia in athletics. *Athletic Training, 18*, 137–138.

Burckes-Miller, M. E., & Black, D. R. (1988a). Eating disorders: A problem in athletics? *Health Education, 19*(1), 22–25.

Burckes-Miller, M. E., & Black, D. R. (1988b). Male and female college athletes: Prevalence of anorexia nervosa and bulimia nervosa. *Athletic Training, 23*, 137–140.

Burckes-Miller, M. E., & Black, D. R. (1991). College athletes and eating disorders: A theoretical context. In D. R. Black (Ed.), *Eating disorders among athletes: Theory, issues, and research* (pp. 11–26). Reston, VA: American Alliance for Health, Physical Education, Recreation and Dance.

Chipman, J. J., Hagan, R. D., Edlin, J. C., Soll, M. H., & Carruth, B. R. (1983). Excessive weight loss in the athletic adolescent: A diagnostic dilemma. *Journal of Adolescent Health Care, 3,* 247–252.

Chopak, J. S., & Taylor-Nicholson, M. (1991). Do female college athletes develop eating disorders as a result of the athletic environment? In D. R. Black (Ed.), *Eating disorders among athletes: Theory, issues, and research* (pp. 87–96). Reston, VA: American Alliance for Health, Physical Education, Recreation and Dance.

Clark, N. (1984). How I manage athletes' food obsessions. *The Physician and Sportsmedicine, 12*(7), 96–103.

Clark, N., Nelson, M., & Evans, W. (1988). Nutrition education for elite female runners. *The Physician and Sportsmedicine, 16*(2), 124–134.

Clement, D. B., & Asmundson, R. C. (1982). Nutritional intake and hematological parameters in endurance runners. *The Physician and Sportsmedicine, 10*(3), 37–43.

Costar, E. D. (1983). Eating disorders: Gymnasts at risk. *International Gymnast, 25*(11), 58–59.

Drewnowski, A., Hopkins, S. A., & Kessler, R. C. (1988). The prevalence of bulimia nervosa in the U.S. college student population. *American Journal of Public Health, 78,* 1322–1324.

Duddle, M. (1973). An increase of anorexia nervosa in a university population. *British Journal of Psychiatry, 123,* 711–712.

Dummer, G. M., Rosen, L. W., Heusner, W. W., Roberts, P. J., & Counsilman, J. E. (1987). Pathogenic weight-control behaviors of young competitive swimmers. *The Physician and Sportsmedicine, 15*(5), 75–84.

Fairbanks, G. (1987). Eating disorders among athletes. *The Physical Educator, 44,* 377–380.

Fairburn, C.G. (1984). Bulimia: Its epidemiology and management. In A. J. Stunkard & E. Stellar (Eds.), *Eating and its disorders* (pp. 235–257). New York: Raven.

Falls, H. B., & Humphrey, L. D. (1978). Body type and composition differences between placers and nonplacers in an AIAW gymnastics meet. *The Research Quarterly, 49,* 38–43.

Folkins, C. H., & Sime, W. E. (1981). Physical fitness training and mental health. *American Psychologist, 36,* 373–389.

Garner, D. M., & Garfinkel, P. E. (1980). Socio-cultural factors in the development of anorexia nervosa. *Psychological Medicine, 10,* 647–656.

Garner, D. M., Garfinkel, P. E., Schwartz, D., & Thompson, M. (1980). Cultural expectations of thinness in women. *Psychological Reports, 47,* 483–491.

Guthrie, S. R. (1991). Prevalence of eating disorders among intercollegiate athletes: Contributing factors and preventative measures. In D. R. Black (Ed.), *Eating disorders among athletes: Theory, issues, and research* (pp. 43–66). Reston, VA: American Alliance for Health, Physical Education, Recreation and Dance.

Halmi, K. (1974). Anorexia nervosa: Demographic and clinical features in 94 cases. *Psychosomatic Medicine, 36,* 18–26.

Hamilton, L. H., Brooks-Gunn, J., Warren, M. P., & Hamilton, W. G. (1988). The role of selectivity in the pathogenesis of eating problems in ballet dancers. *Medicine and Science in Sports and Exercise, 20,* 560–565.

Hansen, N. C. (1978). Wrestling with "making weight?" *The Physician and Sportsmedicine, 6*(4), 106–110.

Humphries, L. L., & Gruber, J. J. (1986). Nutrition behaviors of university majorettes. *The Physician and Sportsmedicine, 14*(11), 91–98.

Hyner, G. C., Melby, C. L., Petosa, R., Seehafer, R., & Black, D. R. (1988). A preferred target population for comprehensive health promotion. *International Quarterly of Community Health Education, 8,* 249–261.

Katz, J. L. (1986). Long-distance running, anorexia nervosa, and bulimia: A report of two cases. *Comprehensive Psychology, 27,* 74–78.

Lindsey, B. J., & Janz, K. F. (1985). A healthy connection: Helping physical educators address eating disorders. *Journal of Physical Education, Recreation and Dance, 56*(9), 41–44.

Lundholm, J. K., & Littrell, J. M. (1986). Desire for thinness among high school cheerleaders: Relationship to disordered eating and weight control behaviors. *Adolescence, 21,* 573–578.

Morgan, W. P. (1985). Affective beneficence of vigorous physical activity. *Medicine and Science in Sports and Exercise, 17,* 94–100.

Nash, H. L. (1987). Do compulsive runners and anorectic patients share common bonds? *The Physician and Sportsmedicine, 15*(12), 162–167.

Overdorf, V. G. (1987). Conditioning for thinness: The dilemma of eating-disordered female athletes. *Journal of Physical Education, Recreation and Dance, 58*(4), 62–65.

Overdorf, V. G. (1991). Eating-related problems in female athletes. In D. R. Black (Ed.), *Eating disorders among athletes: Theory, issues, and research* (pp. 67–86). Reston, VA: American Alliance for Health, Physical Education, Recreation and Dance.

Partin, N. (1988). Internal medicine: Eating disorders and safe weight loss. *Athletic Training, 23,* 47–49.

Romeo, F. (1984). The physical educator and anorexia nervosa. *The Physical Educator, 41,* 2–5.

Rosen, L. W., & Hough, D. O. (1988). Pathogenic weight-control behaviors of female college gymnasts. *The Physician and Sportsmedicine, 16*(9), 140–146.

Ryan, A. J., Gable, D., Tipton, C. M., Morgan, W. P., Lewis, R., & Roy, S. (1981). Weight reduction in wrestling. *The Physician and Sportsmedicine, 9*(9), 78–96.

Schotte, D. E., & Stunkard, A. J. (1987). Bulimia versus bulimic behaviors on a college campus. *JAMA, 258,* 1213–1215.

Shangold, M., Rebar, R. W., Wentz, A. C., & Schiff, I. (1990). Evaluation and management of menstrual dysfunction in athletes. *JAMA, 263,* 1665–1669.

Slavin, J. L. (1987). Eating disorders in athletes. *Journal of Physical Education, Recreation and Dance, 58*(3), 33–36.

Smith, N. J. (1980). Excessive weight loss and food aversions in athletes simulating anorexia nervosa. *Pediatrics, 66,* 139–142.

Smith, N. J. (1984). Weight control in the athlete. *Clinical Sports Medicine, 3,* 693–704.

Smithies, C. S. (1991). Disordered eating behaviors among synchronized swimmers. In D. R. Black (Ed.), *Eating disorders among athletes: Theory, issues, and research* (pp. 111–122). Reston, VA: American Alliance for Health, Physical Education, Recreation and Dance.

Steen, S. N., & McKinney, S. (1986). Nutrition assessment of college wrestlers. *The Physician and Sportsmedicine, 14*(11), 100–116.

Sullivan, K. T., & Steel, D. H. (1991). An exploratory study of eating disorder characteristics among adult female noncollegiate athletes. In D. R. Black (Ed.), *Eating disorders among athletes: Theory, issues, and research* (pp. 123–142). Reston, VA: American Alliance for Health, Physical Education, Recreation and Dance.

Szmukler, G. I., Eisler, I., Gillies, C., & Hayward, M. E. (1985). The implications of anorexia nervosa in a ballet school. *Journal of Psychiatric Research, 19,* 177–181.

Thaxton, L. (1982). Physiological and psychological effects of short-term exercise addiction on habitual runners. *Journal of Sport Psychology, 4,* 73–80.

Thompson, R. A. (1987). Management of the athlete with an eating disorder: Implications for the sport management team. *The Sport Psychologist, 1,* 114–126.

Ubbes, V. A. (1991). Relationship of self-concept, eating behavior, and success of female collegiate gymnasts from Big Ten Conference teams. In D. R. Black (Ed.), *Eating disorders among athletes: Theory, issues, and research* (pp. 143–172). Reston, VA: American Alliance for Health, Physical Education, Recreation and Dance.

Weight, L. M., & Noakes, T. D. (1986). Is running an analog of anorexia? A survey of the incidence of eating disorders in female distance runners. *Medicine and Science in Sports and Exercise, 19,* 213–217.

Wheeler, G. D., Wall, S. R., Belcastro, A. N., Conger, P., & Cumming, D. C. (1986). Are anorexic tendencies prevalent in the habitual runner? *British Journal of Sports Medicine, 20,* 77–81.

Yates, A., Leehey, K., & Shisslak, C. M. (1983). Running—An analogue of anorexia? *New England Journal of Medicine, 308,* 251–255.

Zucker, P., Avener, J., Bayder, S., Brotman, A., Moore, K., & Zimmerman, J. (1985). Eating disorders in young athletes. *The Physician and Sportsmedicine, 13*(11), 88–106.

Author Notes

Preparation of this chapter was supported in part by funds provided to David R. Black from the American Alliance for Health, Physical Education, Recreation and Dance.

We gratefully acknowledge Maureen B. Witt for her contribution to a preliminary draft of this manuscript.

4

Prevalence of Eating Disorders Among Intercollegiate Athletes: Contributing Factors and Preventative Measures

SHARON R. GUTHRIE

Female and male athletes in the sports of cross-country, diving, gymnastics, swimming, synchronized swimming, tennis, track and field, and wrestling (N = 384) were administered the Eating Disorder Inventory, Binge Eating Questionnaire, Purging Mechanism Inventory, and Survey of Eating Disorders Among Athletes. Although instrumentation did not suggest anorexia nervosa as a major health problem, 8% (n = 32) of the athletes were classified as DSM-III bulimic, 41% (n = 159) reported binge eating tendencies, 16% (n = 60) reported purging through vomiting, laxatives, or diuretics, and 23% (n = 89) identified themselves as having a history of eating disorders. With few exceptions, female gymnasts, synchronized swimmers, cross-country runners, swimmers, and divers as well as male wrestlers had higher levels of DSM-III bulimia, binge eating, and self-reported eating disorders than other athletes. In addition, 72% (n = 64) of those who had a history of eating pathology perceived athletic participation as a contributing factor. These data indicate the need for further examination of environmental factors within specific sports that contribute to eating disorders among athletes.

Research over the past three decades has demonstrated a marked increase in eating pathology (i.e., anorexia nervosa, bulimia nervosa) within Western society. Although once considered a rare psychiatric disorder, anorexia is now recognized as a more common phenomenon, particularly among the female population (Bruch, 1973, 1978; Crisp, Palmer, & Kalucy, 1976; Garfinkel & Garner, 1982). Researchers have noted that the prevalence of bulimia nervosa is significantly greater and involves a more heterogeneous group of individuals than anorexia nervosa (Boskind-White & White, 1983; Garner & Olmsted, 1984; Pope, Hudson, & Yurgelun-Todd, 1984).

During the late 1970s and early 1980s, researchers began documenting eating disorders as prevalent among dancers (Druss, 1979; Garner & Garfinkel, 1980; Maloney, 1983; Vincent, 1979), models (Button & Whitehouse, 1981; Garner & Garfinkel, 1980), and Greek sorority members (Cusins & Svendsen, 1980). This research was followed by anecdotal accounts of anorexia and bulimia among elite runners and gymnasts (Folkenberg, 1984; Levin, 1983; McCoy, 1984). Also at this time, researchers and therapists were predicting (Boskind-White & White, 1983; Buickel, 1983; Cauwels, 1983; Garner, Garfinkel, & Olmsted, 1983; Leon, 1984; Mallick, Whipple, & Huerta, 1987; Smith, 1980; Yates, Leehey, & Shisslak, 1983) that athletes were a "high risk" group for developing eating disorders, particularly those involved in sports in which light weight and/or small body size is deemed necessary to achieve performance success (e.g., runners, swimmers, crew members, jockeys), weight classifications apply (e.g., wrestlers, boxers), and/or aesthetic ideals of beauty apply (e.g., figure skaters, gymnasts, synchronized swimmers, divers, body builders).

These predictions stimulated a series of prevalence studies which have produced a wide range of results. While most researchers have reported that eating disordered attitudes and behaviors exist in sport, particularly among women and athletes who participate in sports in which leanness and weight categories are emphasized (Borgen & Corbin, 1987; Burckes-Miller & Black, 1988; Gadpaille, Sanborn, & Wagner, 1987; Guthrie, 1985; Rippon, Nash, Myburgh, & Noakes, 1988; Rosen & Hough, 1988; Rosen, McKeag, Hough, & Curley, 1986; Smithies, 1988; Steen & McKinney, 1986), they have disagreed as to how extensive the problems are and to what degree athletic participation contributes to the problem. For example, Borgen and Corbin (1987) found that athletes were more likely to be weight-preoccupied and have tendencies toward eating disorders than nonathletes. They concluded that athletes in activities that emphasize leanness may be especially at risk due to environmental demands. In contrast, Willis (1986) found not only that eating pathology among athletes was uncommon but also that athletes were less likely than nonathletes to develop an eating disorder. Moreover, 90% of those athletes sampled indicated that participation in sport had helped rather than hindered their problem with food and weight control. Despite current variability in prevalence rates and research findings, most researchers do agree that eating disorders present a serious health problem for some athletes, regardless of gender and sport, and that preventative efforts should be made.

In addition to estimating the prevalence of eating disorders among a randomly selected intercollegiate population and examining specific sport differences, the research reported here was also designed to identify factors within the athletic environment that may have contributed to these eating disorders and preventative measures which may reduce the incidence of eating pathology among athletes.

Method

Subjects

Subjects were 384 intercollegiate men and women participating in the sports of cross-country ($n = 32$, 8%), diving ($n = 8$, 2%), gymnastics ($n = 20$, 5%), swimming ($n = 67$, 18%), synchronized swimming ($n = 17$, 4%), tennis ($n = 58$, 15%), track-field events ($n = 32$, 8%), track-running ($n = 83$, 22%), and wrestling ($n = 67$, 18%) in five universities and colleges in Ohio during the 1984–85 academic year. While these athletes were predominantly Caucasian ($n = 324$, 84%), a relatively small number of Afro-Americans ($n = 43$, 11%), Mexican Americans ($n = 6$, 2%), Asian Americans ($n = 4$, 1%), American Indians ($n = 3$, 1%), and others ($n = 4$, 1%) were also represented. Eighty two percent ($n = 315$) of the sample were first string athletes while 18% classified themselves as second string ($n = 44$) or less ($n = 25$). In terms of grant-in-aid status, 22% ($n = 86$) were playing on a full scholarship, 46% ($n = 174$) on a partial scholarship, and 33% ($n = 124$) with no scholarship. Although the majority of the athletes considered themselves to be of average weight ($n = 236$, 62%), others reported that they were either overweight ($n = 83$, 21%) or underweight ($n = 65$, 17%). In addition, 37% ($n = 141$) reported that they were dissatisfied with their weight at the time of the study.

The five colleges and universities from which the sample was drawn were randomly selected from a frame that included 11 institutions in Ohio. Each sampling unit had a student enrollment greater than 10,000. This selection criterion was used because these institutions were more likely to represent NCAA Division I and II schools and, therefore, have higher levels of competition. An attempt was made to survey all athletes participating in the selected sports. While participation was voluntary, all but 42 athletes were surveyed, which produced a 90% response rate. Of those athletes who did not participate in this study, only 14 (33%) declined to participate. The remaining 28 athletes (67%) were not included as a result of their coach's decision not to participate in this study or failure to return absentee materials on time.

Procedures

The instrument package contained the following questionnaires (see Appendix 4.A), administered in the order presented below:

Eating Disorder Inventory (EDI). The EDI, developed by Garner, Olmsted, and Polivy (1983), is a self-report measure of eight attitudinal and behavioral dimensions associated with anorexia nervosa (i.e., self-inflicted starvation due to severely restrictive dieting, fasting, and often excessive exercise). The instrument consists of 64 items contained within eight six-point, Likert-type scales. The EDI was selected because research and clinical experience have shown the scale to have high utility as a prognostic screening instrument.

Binge Eating Questionnaire (BEQ). The BEQ, developed by Pope et al. (1983), is an eight-item self-report questionnaire designed to assess bulimia (i.e., episodes of binge eating followed by vomiting, laxatives, and/or diuretics) and binge eating (i.e., bouts of uncontrolled overeating which may or may not be followed by dieting, fasting, and/or exercise to prevent weight gain). The BEQ was selected because the instrument measures bulimia according to *DSM-III* criteria (American Psychiatric Association, 1980), that is, (a) recurrent episodes of binge eating; (b) awareness that the eating pattern is abnormal and fear of not being able to stop eating voluntarily; (c) depressed mood and self-deprecating thoughts following eating binges; and (d) at least three of the following: (1) consumption of high caloric, easily ingested food during a binge; (2) inconspicuous eating during a binge; (3) termination of such eating episodes by abdominal pain, sleep, social interruption, or self-induced vomiting; (4) repeated attempts to lose weight by severely restrictive diets, self-induced vomiting, or use of cathartics or diuretics; or (5) frequent weight fluctuations greater than ten pounds due to alternating binges and fasts.

Purging Mechanism Inventory (PMI). The PMI, developed by Guthrie (1985), is an eight-item questionnaire that identifies methods of weight control as well as the frequency with which each method is used (see Appendix 4.B). These methods include diet pills, vomiting, laxatives, diuretics, exercise, severely restrictive dieting (i.e., ingestion of less than 1,000 calories daily), and fasting.

Survey of Eating Disorders Among Athletes (SEDA). The SEDA, developed by Guthrie (1985), is a 33-item questionnaire that identifies the following: (a) the prevalence of eating disorders (i.e., anorexia nervosa, bulimia, binge eating) according to self-identification; (b) factors within the athletic environment that may contribute to these disorders; and (c) preventative measures that may reduce the incidence of eating pathology within the selected sports (see Appendix 4.C).

Validity and Reliability

The instrument package was tested for suitability utilizing a sample of college students ($N = 30$). Two reliability checks were performed on similar items organized according to a given construct within each questionnaire in the instrument package (e.g., a subscale of the EDI, similarly scaled items of the PMI and SEDA). A test-retest over a one week interval with a group of intercollegiate athletes ($N = 30$) demonstrated coefficients of stability for the eight EDI subscales from .71 to .95, the BEQ ($r = .86$), the PMI ($r = .70$ and .90), and the SEDA ($r = .86$, 1.00, and 1.00). Internal consistency was also established for appropriate parts of each questionnaire and produced Cronbach alphas for the EDI from .54 to .92, the BEQ ($\alpha = .83$), the PMI ($\alpha = .70$ and .83), and the SEDA ($\alpha = .50$, .73, and .90).[1]

Criterion-related validity was established for the EDI by comparing EDI anorexic patient profiles ($N = 49$) with the clinical judgments of those familiar with the psychological characteristics of these patients. The correlations between the therapist-consultant ratings and the anorexic patients' self-report subscale scores were all statistically significant ($p < .001$). Criterion-related validity was also established by demonstrating that restricter anorexic subjects could be distinguished from bulimic anorexics as a result of their higher scores on Bulimia and Body Dissatisfaction subscales. Convergent and discriminant validity was established by correlating the subscales with 10 other psychometric instruments that conceptually overlapped the EDI. Correlations produced were impressive and consistent with current formulations regarding anorexia nervosa.[2]

Criterion-related validity for the BEQ was established in that the instrument accurately discriminated between those with clinically diagnosed *DSM-III* bulimia ($n = 20$) and those with no indication of eating disordered behavior ($n = 85$). These findings have suggested a probability of less than .05% that the BEQ would produce a "false negative" and thereby overestimate the prevalence of bulimia.

In that the PMI and the SEDA were created specifically for the purposes of this study, content validity was established by a panel of experts composed of counseling and clinical psychologists ($n = 4, 4\%$), sport psychologists ($n = 2, 2\%$), and physical educators ($n = 4, 4\%$) who had experience with eating disordered athletes. These experts were asked to assess whether or not the questions and scoring procedures seemed adequate and appropriate for collecting the intended data. After incorporating the advised revisions, content validity was established.

---

[1]For complete information on reliability coefficients, contact the author.
[2]For complete table of correlation coefficients, see Garner et al. (1983).

Data Collection and Analysis

The instrument package was administered by the researcher in a group setting. Coaches and other athletic personnel were asked to leave the survey area to minimize any possible coercion to participate. Prior to administration, the nature and importance of the study were explained. In addition, participants were encouraged to be candid in their responses and informed of their right to refuse participation. At the end of each session, they were provided with eating disorder information and local referral sources, as well as encouraged to contact the investigator if they had questions and/or concerns. Those athletes who volunteered to participate were asked to sign a consent form approved by the Protection of Human Subjects Committee of The Ohio State University.

Descriptive statistics were employed to summarize and analyze the data. A t-test and one-way analysis of variance, utilizing Least-Significant Difference (LSD) at $p < .05$ for *a posteriori* contrast, were used to determine significant differences between groups formed on the basis of the gender and type of sport. In order to control for differences in administration, participants who responded during the initial survey sessions were compared to absentees who were later surveyed by mail. No significant differences were observed; therefore, all of the questionnaires were used in the data analysis.

Results

EDI Data

Subscale scores were determined for each respondent ($N = 384$). The means of these subscale scores were then computed to identify the average score for all athletes on each of the eight subscales. Table 4.1 shows the mean subscale scores and standard deviations for all athletes, as well as those for women and men separately. Women scored significantly higher than men on the Drive for Thinness, $t(382) = -9.8$, $p < .001$, Body Dissatisfaction, $t(382) = -9.9$, $p < .001$, and Interoceptive Awareness, $t(382) = -4.8$, $p < .001$ subscales while men scored significantly higher than women on Interpersonal Distrust, $t(382) = 2.3$, $p < .05$ and Maturity Fears, $t(382) = 2.3$, $p < .05$.

Mean subscale scores were used to plot EDI profiles, which allowed a comparison of athlete responses with those of the anorexic ($n = 155$) and college female samples ($n = 271$) used in the Garner et al. (1983)

Table 4.1

Means and Standard Deviations for Different Groups on Each EDI Subscale

EDI Subscale	All athletes (N = 384)		Women (N = 158)		Men (N = 226)	
	M	SD	M	SD	M	SD
1. Drive for Thinness	3.5	4.8	6.1	5.8	1.8	2.7
2. Bulimia	1.8	2.5	1.8	2.5	1.8	2.5
3. Body Dissatisfaction	5.5	6.3	8.9	7.6	3.1	3.8
4. Ineffectiveness	1.4	2.3	1.7	2.6	1.2	2.1
5. Perfectionism	6.3	4.0	6.1	4.4	6.5	3.7
6. Interpersonal Distrust	2.5	2.8	2.2	2.5	2.8	2.9
7. Interoceptive Awareness	2.0	2.9	2.9	3.6	1.3	2.0
8. Maturity Fears	2.5	2.6	2.1	2.4	2.7	2.8

validation study. Shaded areas on each profile figure indicated the 99% confidence intervals for these groups; that is, scores falling within the shaded ranges are not significantly different ($p < .01$) from the respective normative sample means. Figure 4.1 represents the EDI profiles constructed for women and men. Profiles indicated that both groups did not exhibit the psychopathological characteristics of anorexia nervosa in that all subscale scores were below the anorexic range.

Athletes with a score of 14 or greater on the Drive for Thinness subscale were identified as weight-preoccupied. Fourteen represents the mean score of the anorexic group in Garner et al. (1983) and, therefore, is considered indicative of a high degree of concern with weight issues (Garner & Olmsted, 1984). Of the athletes, 7% ($n = 25$) were identified as weight-preoccupied; 24 were females. Table 4.2 shows the frequency and percentage distributions of athletes in each of the sports who were identified as weight-preoccupied. Weight-preoccupation was most frequently distributed among female gymnasts ($n = 3$, 27%), synchronized swimmers ($n = 4$, 24%), and swimmers/divers ($n = 7$, 21%).

BEQ Data

Eight percent ($n = 32$) of the athletes were identified as bulimic according to strict criteria of the *Diagnostic and Statistical Manual of Mental Disorders DSM-III* (American Psychiatric Association, 1980). Gender differences were observed in that 12% ($n = 21$) of the women could be classified as bulimic compared to only 5% ($n = 11$) of the men. Table 4.2 also shows the frequency and percentage distributions of

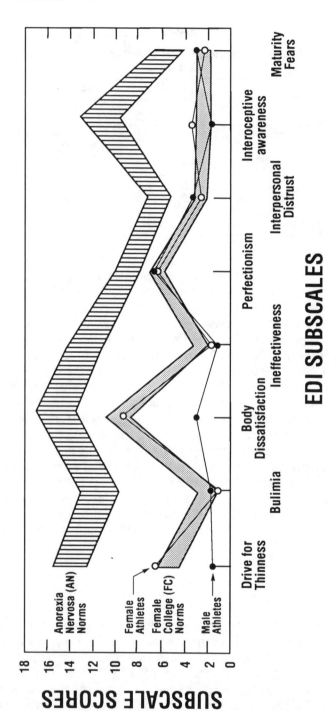

Figure 4.1.   Comparison of EDI norms with male and female athletes.

Table 4.2

Number of Athletes in EDI and BEQ Categories and Number Who Reported Histories of Eating Disorders

Groups	Weight-Preoccupied	DSM-III[a] Bulimia	Binge Eating	Purging	Disorder in Past	Disorder Now
All Participants						
Women (n = 158)	24/15.2	21/13.3	67/42.4	35/22.2	47/30.0	27/17.1
Men (n = 226)	1/ 0.4	11/ 4.9	92/40.7	25/11.0	42/19.0	28/12.4
Women						
Cross-Country (n = 13)	2/15.4	3/23.1	7/53.9	4/30.8	5/38.5	2/15.4
Gymnastics (n = 11)	3/27.3	3/27.3	7/63.7	6/54.6	8/72.7	4/36.4
Swimming/Diving (n = 33)	7/21.1	6/18.2	16/48.5	9/27.3	12/36.2	8/24.2
Synchronized Swimming (n = 17)	4/23.5	4/23.5	7/41.4	6/35.5	7/41.2	3/17.6
Tennis (n = 33)	3/ 9.1	3/ 9.1	12/36.4	4/12.2	5/15.2	4/12.1
Track (Field) (n = 18)	3/16.7	1/ 5.6	5/27.8	1/ 5.6	1/ 5.6	0/ 0.0
Track (Running) (n = 33)	2/ 6.1	1/ 3.0	13/39.4	5/15.2	10/14.9	6/18.2
Men						
Cross-Country (n = 19)	0/ 0.0	0/ 0.0	5/26.4	1/ 5.3	0/ 0.0	0/ 0.0
Gymnastics (n = 9)	0/ 0.0	0/ 0.0	2/22.2	0/ 0.0	0/ 0.0	0/ 0.0
Swimming/Diving (n = 42)	0/ 0.0	0/ 0.0	14/33.3	2/ 4.8	7/16.7	2/ 4.8
Tennis (n = 25)	0/ 0.0	2/ 8.0	8/32.0	1/ 4.0	3/12.0	1/ 4.0
Track (Field) (n = 14)	0/ 0.0	0/ 0.0	2/14.2	0/ 0.0	1/ 7.1	0/ 0.0
Track (Running) (n = 50)	1/ 2.0	2/ 4.0	16/32.0	1/ 2.0	7/14.0	6/12.0
Wrestling (n = 67)	0/ 0.0	7/10.4	35/67.2	20/29.8	23/34.3	19/28.4

Note: The numbers preceding the slash are frequencies. The numbers after the slash are percentages.
[a] Identified as bulimic according to the *Diagnostic and Statistical Manual of Mental Disorders*, 3rd ed. (American Psychiatric Association, 1980) criteria.

athletes participating in different sports who were classified as *DSM-III* bulimic. *DSM-III* bulimia was most frequently distributed among female gymnasts ($n = 3$, 27%), synchronized swimmers ($n = 4$, 24%), cross-country runners ($n = 3$, 23%), and swimmers/divers ($n = 6$, 18%) and among male wrestlers ($n = 7$, 10%).

Forty-one percent ($n = 159$) of the athletes reported binge eating tendencies and 16% ($n = 60$) purged through the use of vomiting, laxatives, and/or diuretics. Table 4.2 shows the frequency and percentage distributions of athletes who binged and purged, as well as those data distributed by sport. While binge eating was equally distributed among women and men, women ($n = 35$, 22%) had a higher percentage distribution of purging than men ($n = 25$, 11%). The highest distributions of binge eating were among female gymnasts ($n = 7$, 64%), cross-country runners ($n = 7$, 54%), swimmers/divers ($n = 16$, 49%), and synchronized swimmers ($n = 7$, 41%) and among male wrestlers ($n = 35$, 67%) and swimmers/divers ($n = 14$, 33%). Similarly, female gymnasts had the highest distribution of purging ($n = 6$, 55%), followed by synchronized swimmers ($n = 6$, 36%), cross-country runners ($n = 4$, 31%), and swimmers/divers ($n = 9$, 27%). Among the male athletes, wrestlers had the highest rates of purging ($n = 20$, 30%).

PMI Data

Table 4.3 shows the frequencies and percentage distributions of athletes who used various methods to control or lose weight at least twice per week, as well as the seasonal basis of severe dieting and fasting. Women were more likely than men to diet and fast to manage weight and to do so throughout the academic year rather than during the athletic season only.

Purging (i.e., vomiting, laxatives, diuretics, diet pills) was not a common practice among the athletes in that more than 80% reported never having used such methods to control weight. Other methods were used, however; 11% ($n = 41$) engaged in severely restrictive dieting or fasting, 47% ($n = 182$) used exercise gained as a regular part of athletic training and competition, and 34% ($n = 129$) combined this with exercise outside the athletic setting.[3]

---

[3]Using the revised *DSM-III-R* criteria for bulimia nervosa (American Psychiatric Association, 1987) that include vigorous exercise, strict dieting, and fasting as purging methods, findings indicate a much higher percentage of athletes using bulimic-like behaviors to prevent weight gain.

SEDA Data

A number of athletes reported that they had an eating disorder, either in the past (n = 89, 23%) or at the time of the study (n = 55, 14%). Of those athletes who reported currently having an eating disorder, the most commonly reported was binge eating (n = 34, 9%) followed by anorexia nervosa (n = 11, 3%) and then bulimia (n = 10, 3%). Eighty-three percent (n = 74) of the athletes who had a history of eating disorders were 18 years of age or younger at the time of onset. More specifically, 69% of them were in high school (n = 41) or college (n = 20) and 31% were either in elementary (n = 11) or junior high/middle school (n = 17).

Of those athletes who had eating disorders in the past (n = 89), 28% believed that athletic participation did not contribute to their eating problems (n = 20). The vast majority (72%, n = 64), however, reported that their eating disorder became more of a problem as a result of athletic participation. The findings were similar for the 55 athletes who reported current eating pathology in that 73% (n = 40) perceived athletic participation as contributing to their eating problems. Table 4.2 shows the frequency and percentage of women and men in each sport who identified themselves as having had eating disorders.

Table 4.3

Frequency and Percentage Distributions of Athletes in Different Groups Who Purge at Least Twice Weekly and Seasonal Basis of Dieting/Fasting

	All Athletes (N = 384)		Women (N = 158)		Men (N = 226)	
	f	%	f	%	f	%
Purging Method						
Diet pills	4	1.1	3	1.9	1	.4
Vomiting	5	1.4	2	1.2	3	1.3
Laxatives	3	.8	1	.6	2	.9
Diuretics	4	1.8	2	1.3	2	.9
Strict dieting/fasting	41	10.7	23	14.5	17	7.5
Exercise out of sport	129	33.6	62	39.2	65	28.7
Exercise part of sport	182	47.4	94	59.5	85	37.7
Seasonal Basis of Severe Diet/Fast						
Preseason only	31	15.7	9	9.5	22	21.4
During season only	63	31.8	12	12.6	51	49.5
Postseason only	14	7.1	7	7.4	7	6.8
Before and during only	29	14.6	16	16.8	13	12.6
Before and after only	20	10.1	16	16.8	4	3.9
During and after only	7	3.5	5	5.3	2	1.9
At all times of the year	34	17.2	30	31.6	4	3.9

As seen in Table 4.2, both gender and sport differences were observed. Women had higher frequency distributions of eating disorders than men, X^2 (1, $N = 384$) = 6.51, $p < .01$. Female gymnasts reported the highest percentages of eating pathology ($n = 8$, 73%), followed by synchronized swimmers ($n = 7$, 41%), cross-country runners ($n = 5$, 39%), and swimmers/divers ($n = 12$, 36%). Among the men, wrestlers ($n = 23$, 34%) and swimmers/divers ($n = 7$, 17%) had the highest distributions.

Athletes who identified themselves as having had eating disorders, either in the past or at the time of the study, were asked to identify factors within the athletic environment that they believed contributed to their eating problems. Level of contribution for each factor was determined on a continuum from "no contribution" (0) to "strong contribution" (9). In addition, all athletes, regardless of whether or not they had an eating disorder, were asked to identify preventative measures that they believed would be helpful in reducing the incidence of eating pathology in sport. Level of helpfulness for each measure was examined on a continuum from "not at all helpful" (0) to "very helpful" (9).

Table 4.4 shows the mean scores of the contributing factors and preventative measures. By far the most important contributing factor was the requirement of weight loss for performance excellence. The major preventative measures mentioned by all athletes were nutritional education and counseling, emphasis on fitness rather than body weight and body fat ideals, sensitivity of athletic personnel to weight control issues, and stress management counseling.

Discussion

The findings of this study indicate that both female and male athletes do not demonstrate anorexic symptomatology; however, additional information indicates that athletes may be at risk in other ways. For example, significant gender differences were observed in that women scored higher on Drive for Thinness, Body Dissatisfaction, and Interoceptive Awareness subscales of the EDI. These findings are congruent with those of Garner et al. (1983). Epidemiological research repeatedly has demonstrated that anorexia nervosa affects primarily women (American Psychiatric Association, 1987; Arenson, 1984; Boskind-Lodahl, 1976, 1977; Gandour, 1984; Garner, Polivy, & Olmsted, 1981; Halmi, Falk, & Schwartz, 1981; Hawkins & Clement, 1980, 1984; Orbach, 1978; Stangler & Printz, 1980). These gender differences may represent variables that increase the vulnerability of women to anorexia nervosa as well as other forms of eating pathology.

Only a small number of the athletes were classified as bulimic according to *DSM-III* criteria; however, larger numbers engaged in binge eating and purging on a regular basis. Again, major gender differences were observed in that almost two-thirds of those classified as *DSM-III* bulimic were women, and women more often used purging to control weight. Sport differences were also observed. With few exceptions, female cross-country runners, gymnasts, swimmers/divers, and syn-

Table 4.4

Mean Scores of Contributing Factors Reported by Athletes Having Had Eating Disorders (N = 89) and Preventative Measures Reported by All Athletes (N = 384)

	Mean
Contributing Factor	
Weight loss was required for performance excellence	5.9
Weight loss was required to reach aesthetic ideals of beauty	4.1
Athletic personnel made remark regarding need for weight loss	3.7
Weight loss was required to meet a lower weight category	3.5
Had to be weighed in front of an audience (e.g., team members)	3.1
Each team member's weight was made public knowledge	2.8
Required to reduce body fat/weight to fit coach's desired ideal	2.8
Feared losing position or team membership if did not lose weight	2.3
Preventative Measures	
Nutritional education and counseling	5.8
Emphasis on fitness rather than body weight and body fat ideals	5.8
Sensitivity of athletic personnel to issues regarding weight control	5.4
Psychological counseling to help deal with stressors of sport	5.3
Consciousness-raising regarding eating disorders	4.9
Less emphasis on meeting lower weight categories	4.5
Policy that athlete will not lose position/team membership if seeks help for eating disorder	4.4
Change in aesthetic ideals of the sport	3.8
Policy that an athlete will be suspended/eliminated from team if reaches a dangerously low body weight	3.6
Policy that athlete with eating disorders cannot play until seeks help	3.5

chronized swimmers, as well as male wrestlers and swimmers/divers reported higher percentages of eating disordered behavior than other athletes. These athletes also tended to have the highest prevalence of *DSM-III* bulimia, as well as the highest percentage distributions of binge eating and purging (i.e., vomiting, laxatives, and diuretics). These findings indicate that further research examining eating disorders among athletes who participate in sports with weight-class categories, speed performance requirements, and strict aesthetic ideals is needed.

Purging was not a common practice among the athletes in this sample in that 83% reported never having used such methods to control weight. Of those who purged to control weight, only a very small percentage reported utilizing such methods on a weekly (6%) or daily (2%) basis. Findings indicated that athletes were more likely to use strict dieting, fasting, and exercise to prevent weight gain. Applying the revised *DSM-III-R* (American Psychiatric Association, 1987) criteria for determining bulimia nervosa, higher percentages of bulimia nervosa and bulimic-like behaviors were evident.

The finding that many athletes reported eating problems before entering college suggests a need to examine the prevalence of eating pathology among younger athletes. Athletes in public schools, as well as in private settings such as private schools, clubs, and sports leagues, should be included. Competition may be most intense during the early years of training (e.g., striving for Olympic candidacy and college scholarships) and thus make the greatest contribution to eating pathology among athletes.

In conclusion, this study indicates that even though anorexia nervosa did not appear to be a major problem, bulimia nervosa and binge eating were common among these athletes, regardless of gender. Significantly, the vast majority of athletes who reported a history of eating pathology perceived that athletic participation contributed to the problem. This finding strongly suggests the need for further examination of factors within the athletic environment that contribute to eating pathology among athletes (e.g., overemphasis on leanness or weight loss, public weigh-ins, insensitive remarks regarding weight made by athletic personnel, weight cutting to fit lower weight categories). The results of this study also indicate that athletes have some awareness of eating pathology and would be receptive to nutritional education and guidance, training emphasizing total fitness and body composition rather than body weight or body fat alone, positive interactions between athletes and athletic personnel on weight control issues, and stress management counseling.

References

American Psychiatric Association. (1980). *Diagnostic and statistical manual of mental disorders* (3rd ed.). Washington, DC: Author.

American Psychiatric Association. (1987). *Diagnostic and statistical manual of mental disorders* (3rd ed., revised). Washington, DC: Author.

Arenson, G. (1984). *Binge eating: How to stop it forever.* New York: Rauson Associates.

Borgen, J. S., & Corbin, C. B. (1987). Eating disorders among female athletes. *The Physician and Sportsmedicine, 15* (2), 89–95.

Boskind-Lodahl, M. (1976). Cinderella stepsisters: A feminist perspective of anorexia nervosa and bulimia. *Signs: Journal of Women in Culture and Society, 2,* 342–356.

Boskind-Lodahl, M. (1977). The definition and treatment of bulimarexia: The gorging/purging syndrome of young women (Doctoral dissertation, Cornell University, 1977). *Dissertation Abstracts International, 38,* 12A.

Boskind-White, M., & White, W. C. (1983). *Bulimarexia: The binge/purge cycle.* New York: W. W. Norton.

Bruch, H. (1973). *Eating disorders.* New York: Basic Books.

Bruch, H. (1978). *The golden cage: The enigma of anorexia nervosa.* Cambridge, MA: Harvard University Press.

Buickel, S. (1983). Anorexia nervosa and bulimia in athletics. *Athletic Training, 18,* 137–138.

Burckes-Miller, M. E., & Black, D. R. (1988). Behaviors and attitudes associated with eating disorders: Perceptions of college athletes about food and weight. *Health Education Research, Theory and Practice, 3,* 203–208.

Button, E. J., & Whitehouse, A. (1981). Subliminal anorexia nervosa. *Psychological Medicine, 11,* 509–516.

Cauwels, J. M. (1983). *Bulimia: The binge-purge compulsion.* New York: Doubleday.

Crisp, A. H., Palmer, R. L., & Kalucy, R. S. (1976). How common is anorexia nervosa? A prevalence study. *British Journal of Psychiatry, 218,* 549–554.

Cusins, J., & Svendsen, D. (1980). *The prevalence of eating disordered attitudes in a sample of female college students, sorority members, and dancers.* Unpublished manuscript, The Ohio State University, Ohio, Student Counseling Center.

Druss, R. G. (1979). Body image and perfectionism of ballerinas: Comparison and contrast with anorexia nervosa. *General Hospital Psychiatry, 1* (2), 115–121.

Folkenberg, J. (1984, March) Bulimia: Not for women only. *Psychology Today,* p. 10.

Gadpaille, W. J., Sanborn, C. F., & Wagner, W. W. (1987). Athletic amenorrhea, major affective disorders, and eating disorders. *American Journal of Psychiatry, 144,* 939–942.

Gandour, M. J. (1984). Bulimia: Clinical description, assessment, etiology, and treatment. *International Journal of Eating Disorders, 3,* 3–38.

Garfinkel, P. E., & Garner, D. M. (1982). *Anorexia nervosa: A multidimensional perspective.* New York: Brunner/Mazel.

Garner, D. M., & Garfinkel, P. E. (1980). Sociocultural factors in the development of anorexia nervosa. *Psychological Medicine, 10,* 647–656.

Garner, D. M., Garfinkel, P. E., & Olmsted, M. P. (1983). An overview of sociocultural factors in the development of anorexia nervosa. In *Anorexia nervosa: Recent development in research.* New York: Alan R. Liss.

Garner, D. M., Olmsted, M. P., & Polivy, J. (1983). Development and validation of a multidimensional eating disorder inventory for anorexia nervosa and bulimia. *International Journal of Eating Disorders, 2,* 15–34.

Garner, D. M., Olmsted, M. P., & Polivy, J. (1984). *Manual for eating disorder inventory (EDI).* Odessa, FL: Psychological Assessment Resources, Inc.

Garner, D. M., Polivy, J., & Olmsted, M. P. (1981, August). *Anorexia nervosa, obesity, and dietary chaos: Common and distinctive features.* Paper presented at the annual meeting of the American Psychological Association, Los Angeles, CA.

Guthrie, S. R. (1985). The prevalence and development of eating disorders within a selected intercollegiate athlete population. *Dissertation Abstracts International, 46,* 3649A–3650A. (University Microfilms No. AD G86-03006, 8606).

Halmi, K. A., Falk, J. R., & Schwartz, E. (1981). Binge-eating and vomiting: A survey of a college population. *Psychological Medicine, 11,* 697–706.

Hawkins, R. C., & Clement, P. F. (1980). Development and construct validation of a self-report measure of binge eating tendencies. *Addictive Behaviors, 5,* 219–226.

Hawkins, R. C., & Clement, P. F. (1984). Binge eating: Measurement problems and a conceptual model. In R. C. Hawkins, W. J. Fremouw, & P. F. Clement (Eds.), *The binge-purge syndrome: Diagnosis, treatment and research.* New York: Springer Publishing Co.

Leon, G. (1984). Anorexia nervosa and sports activities. *Behavior-Therapist, 7,* 9–10.

Levin, E. (1983, August 22). A lethal quest for the winning edge. *People Magazine,* pp. 19–22.

Mallick, M. J., Whipple, T. W., & Huerta, E. (1987). Behavioral and psychological traits of weight conscious teenagers: A comparison of eating disordered patients and high and low risk groups. *Adolescence, 22,* 157–168.

Maloney, M. J. (1983). Anorexia nervosa and bulimia in dancers: Accurate diagnosis and treatment planning. *Clinical Sport Medicine, 2,* 549–555.

McCoy, C. R. (1984, August 13). A one time Olympic gymnast overcomes the bulimia that threatened her life. *People Weekly*, pp. 68–70.

Orbach, S. (1978). *Fat is a feminist issue*. New York: Berkley Books.

Pope, H. G., Hudson, J. I., & Yurgelun-Todd, D. (1983). *The development of an instrument to measure DSM-III bulimia*. Unpublished manuscript.

Pope, H. G., Hudson, J. I., & Yurgelun-Todd, D. (1984). Anorexia nervosa and bulimia among 300 suburban women shoppers. *American Journal of Psychiatry, 141*, 292–293.

Rippon, C., Nash, J., Myburgh, K. H., & Noakes, T. D. (1988). Abnormal eating attitude test scores predict menstrual dysfunction in lean females. *International Journal of Eating Disorders, 7*, 617–624.

Rosen, L. W., & Hough, D. O. (1988). Pathogenic weight-control behaviors of female college gymnasts. *The Physician and Sportsmedicine, 16* (9), 140–146.

Rosen, L. W., McKeag, D. B., Hough, D. O., & Curley, V. (1986). Pathogenic weight-control behavior in female athletes. *The Physician and Sports Medicine, 14* (1), 79–86.

Smith, N. J. (1980). Excessive weight loss and food aversion in athletes simulating anorexia nervosa. *Pediatrics, 66*, 139–142.

Smithies, C. S. (1988). Prevalence and correlates of eating disordered behavior among synchronized swimming athletes (Doctoral dissertation, The Ohio State University, 1988). *Dissertation Abstracts International, 50*, 02B.

Stangler, R. S., & Printz, A. M. (1980). DSM-III psychiatric diagnosis in a university population. *American Journal of Psychiatry, 137*, 937–940.

Steen, S. N., & McKinney, S. (1986). Nutrition assessment of college wrestlers. *The Physician and Sportsmedicine, 14* (11), 100–116.

Vincent, L. M. (1979). *Competing with the sylph: Dancers and the pursuit of the ideal body form*. Kansas City: Andrews and McNeel.

Willis, L. R. (1986). Eating disorders and the female athlete (Doctoral dissertation, Brigham Young University, 1986). *Dissertation Abstracts International, 47*, 10A.

Yates, A., Leehey, K., & Shisslak, C. M. (1983). Running: An analogue of anorexia? *The New England Journal of Medicine, 308*, 251–255.

Appendix 4.A

Contents of Guthrie Instrument

Items	Test
1–50	EDI
51–72	BEQ
73–80	PMI
81–113	SEDA

Appendix 4.B

Purging Mechanisms Inventory (PMI)

Another important purpose of this study is to learn about some of the ways in which athletes control or lose weight. The following questions are intended to gather this information. Again, answer by responding with the number that best applies to you.

	Never	Less Than Once a Month	1–3 Times a Month	Once a Week	2–6 Times a Week	Once a Day	More Than Once a Day
73. To what extent do you use *diet pills* to control or lose weight?	0	1	2	3	4	5	6
74. How often do you use *vomiting* to control or lose weight?	0	1	2	3	4	5	6
75. To what extent do you use *laxatives* to control or lose weight?	0	1	2	3	4	5	6
76. How often do you use *diuretics* to control or lose weight?	0	1	2	3	4	5	6

77. How often do you engage in *severely restrictive dieting (less than 1000 calories per day)* or *fasting* to control or lose weight? ⟶ If NEVER, skip to question #79

0 NEVER
1 RARELY
2 OCCASIONALLY
3 FREQUENTLY
4 ALWAYS

Appendix Table 4.B continued here broadside (tb5)

78. During what seasons of the athletic year do you engage in *severely restrictive dieting or fasting to control or lose weight?*

    0   ONLY DURING PRESEASON
    1   ONLY DURING ACTUAL SEASON
    2   ONLY DURING POSTSEASON
    3   BOTH BEFORE AND DURING SEASON BUT NOT AFTER SEASON
    4   BOTH BEFORE AND AFTER SEASON BUT NOT DURING SEASON
    5   BOTH DURING AND AFTER SEASON BUT NOT BEFORE SEASON
    6   AT ALL TIMES DURING THE YEAR

79. To what extent do you use exercise *(not including exercise done as a part of practice sessions or competitive games)* to control or lose weight?

    0   NEVER
    1   RARELY
    2   OCCASIONALLY
    3   FREQUENTLY
    4   ALWAYS

80. How often do you use exercise gained in practice sessions and competitive games to control or lose weight?

    0   NEVER
    1   RARELY
    2   OCCASIONALLY
    3   FREQUENTLY
    4   ALWAYS

Appendix 4.C
Survey of Eating Disorders Among Athletes (SEDA)

As you may know, researchers have found that eating disorders are a common phenomenon in our society. This section of questions is an attempt to determine if this is true within the athlete population. These eating disorders have been classified into the following categories:

Anorexia Nervosa-Restricting Type—This is characterized by self-induced starvation caused by severely restrictive dieting, fasting, and/or excessive exercise. Individuals with restricting anorexia take on an extremely thin or emaciated appearance.

Anorexia Nervosa-Bulimic Type—This also is a form of self-inflicted starvation. These individuals practice food denial (as does the restricter anorexic) but regularly binge eat. In order to eliminate the food, they use any or all of the following purging methods: vomiting, laxatives, diuretics (water pills), diet pills, excessive exercise. They also have an extremely thin or emaciated appearance.

Bulimia—This involves episodes of binge eating followed by some compensatory method(s) for eliminating the food. These methods usually include vomiting, laxatives, and/or diuretics. These individuals may be any weight; however, they tend to fall within the low-normal to high-normal weight range.

Binge Eating—This behavior is characterized by episodes of uncontrolled overeating which may or may not be followed by any or all of the following methods for controlling weight gain: dieting, fasting, and/or exercise. These individuals may be any weight; however, if they do not use some method for controlling or losing weight, they may tend to be overweight or obese.

Please answer the following questions as honestly as possible by marking in the number on your answer sheet that most closely applies to you. *Your answers are strictly confidential!*

81. Do you believe that you *have ever had* an eating disorder? ⟶ If NO, skip to question #87

    0 NO
    1 YES

82. Which type do you believe that you *have had?*

    0 ANOREXIA NERVOSA-RESTRICTING TYPE
    1 ANOREXIA NERVOSA-BULIMIC TYPE
    2 BULIMIA
    3 BINGE EATING

83. How old were you when your eating disorder first began?

    0 12 YEARS OF AGE OR YOUNGER
    1 13–15 YEARS OLD
    2 16–18 YEARS OLD
    3 19 YEARS OF AGE OR OLDER

84. At what level in school were you when your eating disorder first began?

    0 ELEMENTARY SCHOOL
    1 MIDDLE OR JUNIOR HIGH SCHOOL
    2 SENIOR HIGH SCHOOL
    3 COLLEGE

85. Were you participating in sport or athletics at the time when your eating disorder first began?

    0 NO ————————————————→ If NO, skip to question #87
    1 YES

86. To what extent do you believe that your athletic participation *at that time* contributed to your eating disorder?

    0 NOT AT ALL. MY ATHLETIC PARTICIPATION HAD NOTHING TO DO WITH MY EATING DISORDER.
    1 MY EATING DISORDER BECAME LESS OF A PROBLEM AS A RESULT OF MY ATHLETIC PARTICIPATION.
    2 ATHLETIC PARTICIPATION MADE MY EATING DISORDER SOMEWHAT MORE OF A PROBLEM.
    3 ATHLETIC PARTICIPATION MADE MY EATING DISORDER MUCH MORE OF A PROBLEM.
    4 IF I HAD NOT PARTICIPATED IN SPORT OR ATHLETICS AT THE TIME, I PROBABLY WOULD NOT HAVE HAD AN EATING DISORDER.

87. Do you believe that you *now* have an eating disorder?

    0 NO ————————————————→ If NO, skip to question #103 unless
    1 YES   you answered question #86 with a
                                           2, 3, or 4, then skip to question #95

Continued on next page

88. Which type do you think that you *now* have?

   0   ANOREXIA NERVOSA-RESTRICTING TYPE
   1   ANOREXIA NERVOSA-BULIMIC TYPE
   2   BULIMIA
   3   BINGE EATING

89. To what extent do you believe that your *current* athletic participation in intercollegiate sport has contributed to your eating disorder?

   0   NOT AT ALL. MY ATHLETIC PARTICIPATION HAS HAD NOTHING TO DO WITH MY EATING DISORDER.
   1   MY EATING DISORDER HAS BECOME LESS OF A PROBLEM.
   2   ATHLETIC PARTICIPATION HAS MADE MY EATING DISORDER SOMEWHAT MORE OF A PROBLEM.
   3   ATHLETIC PARTICIPATION HAS MADE MY EATING DISORDER MUCH MORE OF A PROBLEM.
   4   IF I DID NOT PARTICIPATE IN ATHLETICS NOW, I PROBABLY WOULD NOT HAVE AN EATING DISORDER.

Please respond to each item below by marking in a number on your answer sheet that best represents your level of agreement according to the following 10-point scale:

0	1	2	3	4	5	6	7	8	9
Strongly Disagree		D I S A G R E E		Slightly Disagree	Slightly Agree		A G R E E		Strongly Agree

90. My eating disorder is related to pressures from school.

91. My eating disorder is related to pressures from home or family.

92. My eating disorder is related to pressures from athletic participation.

93. My eating disorder is related to problems in personal relationships.

94. My eating disorder does not seem to be related to any particular thing or things.

Certain factors within the athletic environment may contribute to the onset or development of eating disorders. Please indicate *to what extent each of the following factors have contributed to your eating disorder* by marking in the appropriate number on your answer sheet from the 10-point scale below:

0	1	2	3	4	5	6	7	8	9
NO CONTRIBUTION					MODERATE CONTRIBUTION				STRONG CONTRIBUTION

95. Weight loss was required for performance excellence.

96. Weight loss was required to meet a lower weight category.

97. Weight loss was required to reach aesthetic ideals of beauty.

98. A member of the athletic personnel (for example: coach, trainer, sport psychologist) made a remark concerning my need for weight loss.

99. I had to be weighed in front of an audience (for example: other team members).

100. Each team member's weight was made public knowledge.

101. I was required to reduce my level of body fat in accordance with the coach's (or other member of the athletic personnel) desired ideal.

102. I was fearful of losing a position on the team or of being kicked off the team if I did not control or lose weight.

⟶ On the sheet of paper provided along with your answer sheet, please list any other *factors within the athletic environment which may have contributed to your eating disorder.* Rate each factor with a number according to the same 10-point scale above.

103. How common do you believe eating disorders are *in your particular sport?*

    0 I DO NOT KNOW
    1 NOT AT ALL COMMON
    2 SOMEWHAT COMMON
    3 VERY COMMON

Continued on next page

Listed in this section are measures which might be taken by those in charge of the athletic program in an attempt to prevent or reduce eating disorders. Please indicate to what extent each of these measures would be helpful in reducing the incidence of eating disorders in your particular sport. Mark in the number on your answer sheet that best applies according to the following 10-point scale:

0	1	2	3	4	5	6	7	8	9
NOT AT ALL HELPFUL					MODERATELY HELPFUL				VERY HELPFUL

104. Nutritional education and counseling both before and during the athletic season.

105. Consciousness-raising regarding eating disorders (for example: their origin, development, and dangers).

106. Emphasis on fitness rather than body weight and body fat ideals.

107. Athletic personnel being sensitive to issues regarding weight control and dieting.

108. Change(s) in the aesthetic (beauty) ideals of the sport.

109. Less emphasis on meeting lower weight categories in the sport.

110. Psychological counseling available before and during the athletic season to help deal with the stresses of my sport.

111. Athletic policy which states that an athlete will be eliminated or suspended from a team if he or she reaches such a low body weight that it becomes dangerous to health and level of wellness.

112. Athletic policy which states that those with eating disorders will not be allowed to play until they seek help.

113. Athletic policy which states that one will not be kicked off a team or lose a position on a team if he or she seeks help for an eating disorder.

→ On the separate sheet provided, please list any other preventative measures which you think might help reduce the incidence of eating disorders in your particular sport. Rate each measure according to the same 10-point scale above.

Author Notes

Preparation of this chapter was supported in part by the American Alliance for Health, Physical Education, Recreation and Dance.

5

Eating Related Problems in Female Athletes

VIRGINIA G. OVERDORF

This study investigated the use of aberrant weight control procedures and eating patterns among 102 female athletes. An eating patterns survey (Eating Patterns of Athletes) was administered to female athletes participating on a variety of team sports with a response rate of 95%. Athletes' perceptions of their weight was almost a mirrored image of their actual weight. Two goodness-of-fit chi-squared tests indicated that how athletes viewed their own weight status as well as how they perceived others to judge them significantly differed from their body mass index categories based on their reported weight, p < .001. Athletes reported that their coaches rarely spoke to them about weight control, in spite of their distinct body image distortions, and also reported use of several types of pathogenic weight control methods; 41% indicated use of at least one pathogenic method. The overwhelming reason reported for their sports participation was to have fun. Body image and pathogenic weight control methods related to the findings are discussed as an exigent problem for the athletic community.

The current rise in the incidence of eating disorders among women in our society is cause for concern (Mitchell & Eckert, 1987). Anorexia nervosa and bulimia nervosa, predominately (but not exclusively) female disorders (Anderson, 1983; Friedrichs, 1988), have been identified as major contemporary concerns for high school and college students (Hesse-Biber, 1989; Peters, Swassing, Butterfield, & McKay, 1984). Thus, it should not be surprising that girls and women who participate in sports may also be prone to eating disorders or aberrant eating behaviors. Yet the problems related to eating habits and weight loss are frequently ignored by practitioners. Inattention to these problems may be related to the fact that aberrant behaviors have not been recognized as serious; or perhaps, the problem is perceived as primarily a female issue that affects only a small proportion of athletes. It should be noted too that aberrant weight control and eating habits are often difficult to detect, especially without formal training, because athletes often conceal such problems. It is probable that any or all of these, as well as other explanations, are true; however, the problems can no longer be ignored, and prevention and treatment programs seem to be an exigent priority for the athletic community.

Distorted body image is one characteristic that could contribute to undesirable weight loss behavior. The diet industry's ubiquitous message that "thin is in" has led many women to quip, but also believe, "you can never be too thin." Some women, perhaps struggling with their own identity and sexuality, take that suggestion to heart. The mirror's reflection is always seen as *too fat*, a condition that can lead to pathogenic weight control practices and eating related problems. While men are undoubtedly affected by the media blitz, women appear to be especially vulnerable. Historically, women have been forced to adapt to cultural fluctuations of aesthetics and style (Aimez, 1983), and the results of such pressure are often manifested at an early age. Recently, it has been estimated that two-thirds of adolescent girls are trying to lose weight (Rosen & Gross, 1987), and a simple diet to lose weight can sometimes evolve into an eating disorder (Overdorf, 1990). Some women have been observed to suffer distortions of body image and emotional disturbances that were manifested in aberrant or self-destructive eating patterns (Anderson, 1983; Knortz & Reinhart, 1984; Steiner-Adair, 1988–89). The cultural fashion for thinness is clearly a background factor for the epidemic of eating disorders currently prevalent among women.

Many eating disordered women have been known to also engage in vigorous, excessive exercise to *carve* more weight from an already emaciated frame (Epling, Pierce, & Stefan, 1983). Could some women participate in athletics to fulfill their drive for excessive exercise? When these girls and women do engage in organized athletic programs, where added rather than reduced calories are needed for the increase in energy demands, their problems could become exacerbated. Coaches who recognize these problems and communicate healthy weight control practices to their athletes are in a favorable position to assist in early intervention and prevention.

How pervasive are eating related problems in athletics? Previous studies over the last decade have identified which sports appear to provide an affinity for women with food related problems. Due to the extreme influence of weight on performance, it is not surprising that an alarming number of gymnasts with disordered eating habits have been identified (Calabrese, 1985; Falls & Humphrey, 1978; Short & Short,

1983). Other activities in which pathogenic means of weight control are prevalent are swimming (Dummer, Rosen, Heusner, Roberts, & Counsilman, 1987), dancing (Maloney, 1983; Szmukler, Eisler, Gillies, & Hayward, 1985), and long distance running (Blumenthal, O'Toole, & Chang, 1984; Katz, 1986). Yet are these the only sports in which these afflicted athletes participate? An NCAA-produced video (Hand, 1989) suggests that no sport is exempt. The increase of women in general with eating problems (Halmi, Falk, & Schwartz, 1981; Levenkron, 1982; Mitchell & Eckert, 1987) may result in eating disordered female athletes participating in sports heretofore exempt from such problems. Are coaches and other sport management personnel prepared to handle the special problems these athletes present?

One step in addressing the prevalence and pervasiveness of eating disorders among female athletes would be to investigate whether female athletes from a broader spectrum of sports would demonstrate difficulties with body image, weight control, and food-related problems. Gathering that type of information, along with whether coaches were communicating with athletes about these topics, was the primary objective of this study. Burckes-Miller and Black (1988b) suggested that the prevalence of college athletes with eating disorder symptoms may exceed that found in society. Another purpose of this study was to evaluate the findings of Burckes-Miller and Black when high school athletes were included.

Method

Subjects

Participants in this study were female athletes ($N = 102$) from high school teams in the Wayne, New Jersey Public Schools and various college teams throughout New York, New Jersey, and Massachusetts. The high school athletes comprised 44% ($n = 45$) of the sample, while the remaining 56% ($n = 57$) were college students. Three-quarters ($n = 77$) of the participants ranged from high school juniors to college juniors, the primary years during which eating disorders are noted to be most common (Yager, 1988). The sample was comprised of athletes participating on the following teams during survey administration: basketball (24.4%, $n = 25$); cross-country (18.5%, $n = 19$); gymnastics (6.9%, $n = 7$); soccer (3%, $n = 3$); swimming (16.6%, $n = 17$); tennis (5%, $n = 5$); track (11.6%, $n = 12$); and volleyball (14%, $n = 14$).

Subjects participated according to whether their coach would permit the team's involvement, and whether they wished to do so; 95% of the targeted subjects completed the survey. The high school athletes were selected from a middle- to upper-class school district. The college athletes were selected from a combination of private and public four-year institutions in the Northeast.

Procedure

Questionnaire Administration. There was a coordinator in each institution who contacted coaches to request their participation. Instructions for administration of the survey were given by the coordinator to the coaches. The instructions underscored the importance of athletes participating voluntarily and emphasized that participation could cease at any time. Furthermore, athletes' participation was to be anonymous, and the coach was instructed to permit athletes to hand in completed surveys collectively and in a fashion that preserved anonymity. Upon collection, the surveys were returned immediately to the institutional coordinator who forwarded them to the investigator. All data were gathered during the fall semester of 1989.

Instrument. The questionnaire used in this survey was based on the "Eating Habits of Athletes" (EHA) questionnaire developed by Burckes-Miller and Black (1988a). Because all of the issues deemed important in this study were not addressed by the EHA, the final questionnaire resulted from a modification in the EHA. The readability and clarity of this questionnaire was assessed by administering it to a group of undergraduate students in a Psychology of Motor Learning class ($n = 25$). Their written and verbal feedback was used to revise the initial document. As in the EHA, the final format involved multiple choice questions, with multiple responses permitted on several items (see Appendix 5.A).

Data Analysis

The findings reported in this study are based on frequency counts of the survey items. The exceptions were the calculation of Body Mass Index (BMI) and chi-squared tests comparing BMI scores to the responses on items pertaining to how athletes perceived their own weight as well as their reports on how others perceived their weight. BMI, or Quetelet index, is a ratio of height to weight, and is calculated by dividing weight in kg by height in m squared. The BMIs calculated were derived from the respondents' reported height and weight, not an actual measurement. Clearly, using reported measures could be a source of error. A possible tendency to "regress toward the mean" in reporting weight, however, should not undermine the findings in this study; it may have actually inflated them. The resulting BMIs were grouped into five categories corresponding to the categories utilized in athletes' perceptions of themselves and others' perceptions of them.

Results

Body Image

When asked about how they perceive their own weight, 3.9% ($n = 4$) of the athletes saw themselves as "much too heavy," 49% ($n = 50$) as "a little heavy," 38.2% ($n = 39$) as "just right," 6.9% ($n = 7$) as "a little thin," while none saw themselves as "much too thin"; 2% ($n = 2$) did not respond to this question. However, when asked how they thought others would perceive their weight, 59.8% ($n = 61$) thought others would see them as "just right." The remainder were fairly well distributed among "a little heavy" (17.6%, $n = 18$) and "a little thin" (15.6%, $n = 16$), while 1% ($n = 1$) thought that others might perceive them as "much too heavy" and 2% ($n = 2$) thought that others might perceive them as "much too thin"; (3.9%, $n = 4$ did not respond).

A BMI score between 20–25 was defined as within the normal range for women. Therefore, those scores were chosen to correspond with the "just right" category. Scores between 25 and 26 were defined as "a little too heavy," while anything above 26 would be "much too heavy." Conversely, 19–20 was the "a little too thin" category, while anything below 19 was rated as "much too thin." While these categories are somewhat arbitrary, they do correspond with categories used by Moriarty and Moriarty (1988) to evaluate athletes.

Interestingly, BMI scores from reported weight indicated that 55% ($n = 56$) of the female athletes in this sample were "just right," 15% ($n = 15$) a "little thin," while 26% ($n = 26$) were "much too thin." A small 1.5% ($n = 2$) were "much too heavy" and a "little heavy"; 3.9% ($n = 3$) did not report their weight. The comparisons of percept and reality (as indicated by the BMI score) of their bodies may be seen in Figure 5.1 As the graph indicates, the athletes' self-perceptions differ markedly from reality and their perceptions of how they think others see them. In fact, a goodness-of-fit chi-squared test indicated that self-

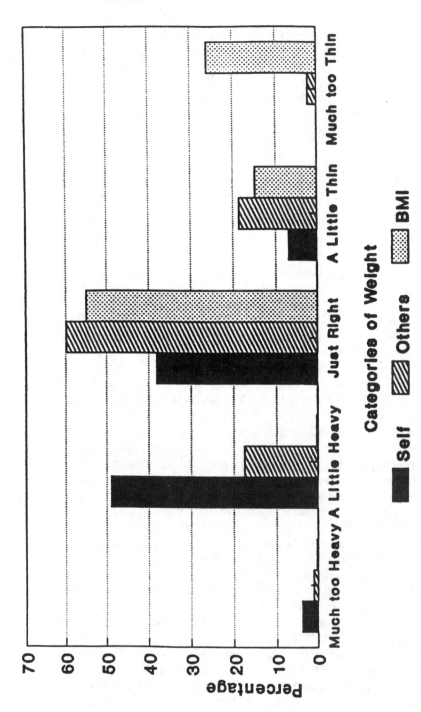

Figure 5.1.   Athletes' BMIs, self-perceptions, and perceptions of how others see them.

perceptions significantly differed from observed BMI scores, $X^2(2, N=100) = 49.86$, $p < .001$. The top three categories were combined because of the small observed values. Furthermore, there was also a significant difference between how they reported others viewed them and BMI scores, $X^2(2, N=98) = 20.17$, $p < .001$.

Coach/Athlete Communications

Another objective from this survey was to identify athletes' perceptions of their coaches' communication on issues of weight control. Asked whether their coach monitored their weight, 62.7% ($n=64$) said "never," 5.8% ($n=6$) said "sometimes," while 27.5% ($n=28$) responded "frequently"; approximately 3.9% ($n=4$) did not respond. They were also asked how often the coach spoke to the team about weight control. Almost 53.9% ($n=55$) said "never," 20.6% ($n=21$) "sometimes," 16.7% ($n=17$) "frequently," and 6.9% ($n=7$) said their coaches constantly stressed weight control to the team; about 2% ($n=2$) did not respond. The question about team communication was followed by a question to determine whether their coach had ever talked to them individually about weight problems. Approximately 76.5% ($n=78$) claimed their coach had never spoken to them personally about their weight. About 8.8% ($n=9$) said their coach had spoken to them about their weight once, 11.8% ($n=12$) "several times," and 2% ($n=2$) said their coaches constantly stressed weight control to them.

There are some clear concerns suggested from these data about communication. First, if 36% of the coaches are monitoring athletes' weight, and 76% are never speaking to their athletes individually about weight issues, what are those other 12% who are monitoring weight doing with that information? Second, and of even greater concern, athletes reported that approximately 46% of the coaches discussed weight control with the team, but only 22.3% of the coaches talked individually to the athletes. These concerns need further examination. Moreover, they suggest a possible need to help coaches become better informed about eating disorders and how to communicate and discuss sensitive topics with athletes such as eating habits and weight loss.

Reasons for Participation in Sport

Reasons athletes reported for participation in sports were also explored in this study and are visually displayed in Figure 5.2. On a multiple response item, athletes were asked to identify reasons that

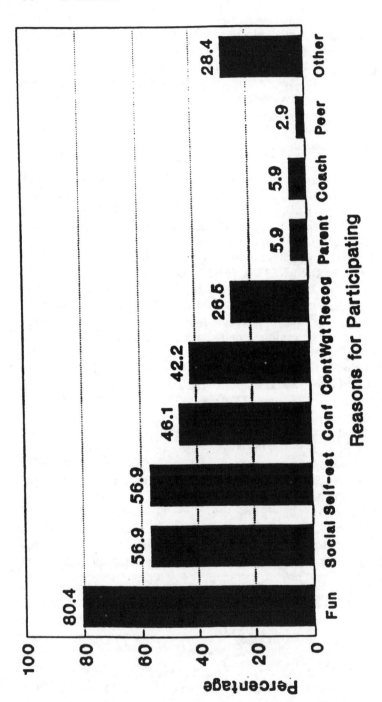

Figure 5.2. Reasons female athletes give for participating in sports.

explained their participation. More than three-quarters of the athletes played to have fun and over half participated for socialization (Social) and to gain self-esteem (Self-est). Pressure from parents, coaches, and peers was reported by the fewest athletes. Other reasons supplied by the athletes were that they were on scholarship, or that they participated for "pure love of the sport."

Thoughts about Food and Weight

When the athletes in this study were asked if they thought they might have an eating disorder, 93.1% ($n = 95$) of them resoundingly said "no," 3.9% ($n = 4$) answered affirmatively, and 2.9% ($n = 3$) did not respond. However, when they were asked if they had ever been diagnosed with an eating disorder, surprisingly, 5.9% ($n = 6$) said "yes," anorexia; 2% ($n = 2$) said "yes," bulimia nervosa; while 89.2% ($n = 91$) said no; 2.9% ($n = 3$) did not respond. Yet these athletes who have been diagnosed with eating disorders, or others who may have food-related problems, apparently did not feel they were properly treated. When the athletes were asked if they had ever had professional counseling, 91% ($n = 93$) said "never," while 5% ($n = 5$) had one visit, 1% ($n = 1$) several visits, 1% ($n = 1$) went regularly, and 2% ($n = 2$) admitted to being afraid to go.

Further insight is gained by looking at the participants' thoughts and activities. Asked about their greatest weight fluctuation over the past year, 6.9% ($n = 7$) exceeded 16 lb weight fluctuations, 6.9% ($n = 7$) fluctuated between 13–15 lb, 12.7% ($n = 13$) varied 10–12 lb, 20.6% ($n = 21$) 7–9 lb, while 52.9% ($n = 54$) reported fluctuations of 6 lb or less. Over one-quarter of these athletes had substantial weight fluctuations during the year preceding survey administration. Because the BMIs indicated that this sample was relatively thin, these weight fluctuations could be of concern, especially coupled with other information they provided about weight control and eating habits.

In response to how often they ate small quantities of food, defined as 600 calories or less, 52.9% ($n = 54$) said "never," 16.7% ($n = 17$) "rarely," 10.8% ($n = 11$) two days/month, 8.8% ($n = 9$) one day/week, while 6.9% ($n = 7$) admitted to, essentially, *starving* themselves two or more days/week; 3.9% ($n = 4$) did not answer. It is important to keep in mind that this information was collected during the competitive season when the caloric demands for these athletes presumably increased. Congruent with women's preoccupation with weight, these female athletes displayed similar obsessive behavior. About 2.9% ($n = 3$) admitted they couldn't stop thinking about their weight, 14.7% ($n = 15$) responded that they thought about their weight "all the time," 35.3% ($n = 36$) quite a lot, 37.6% (n = 37.3) sometimes, while only 8.8% (n = 9) hardly ever thought about weight.

How do these thoughts about weight transfer into activity for these female athletes? Of the entire sample, 41% (n = 42) used one or more pathogenic means of weight control. In a multiple response question, they were asked to identify any means they used for weight control. Figure 5.3 shows the actual percentages of female athletes responding to each of the pathogenic categories. As can be seen, vigorous, excessive exercise (VigExer) was most frequently used, followed closely by fad diets (FadDiet), fasting (Fast), and then diet pills (DietPills). Least frequently used were commercially purchased aids (C."Aids") and self-induced vomiting (SIndVom).

As one final indicator of possible difficulties regarding eating problems, these athletes were asked to respond "yes" or "no" to other items known to be associated with eating disorders. One-fifth (n = 21) of the athletes were actually depressed after they ate, while close to one-sixth (n = 16) didn't like to eat in the presence of others. Missing menstrual cycles can also be symptomatic of eating disorders, and 14.7% (n = 15) had missed three or more consecutive cycles. Clearly, this sample contains some athletes with eating disorder symptomology, who may be on the verge of developing more serious problems.

Discussion

The women in this study primarily participated in sports to have fun. Yet many of these supposedly *fun-seeking* young women have distorted body images. A little over half of the athletes saw themselves as heavy, while in reality only 3% might be categorized on the heavy side. Furthermore, the percentage using pathogenic weight control methods, including exercise abuse, approached half of the sample. These findings may, in fact, be conservative estimates. Employing a procedure whereby coaches collected the surveys may have violated a sense of anonymity for some of these athletes and thereby distorted the findings. Even if this is the case, these data exceed prior prevalence reports by Dummer et al. (1987) of 15.4% and Rosen, McKeag, Hough, & Curley (1986) of 32%. It is important to note that Dummer's results were based on swimmers while Rosen's sample included, predominantly, gymnasts and distance runners. The present data support those of Burckes-Miller and Black (1988b) who found the number of college students meeting the criteria for anorexia to be 1 in 33, and for bulimia approximately 1 in 5. (It should be noted that the Burckes-Miller and Black study

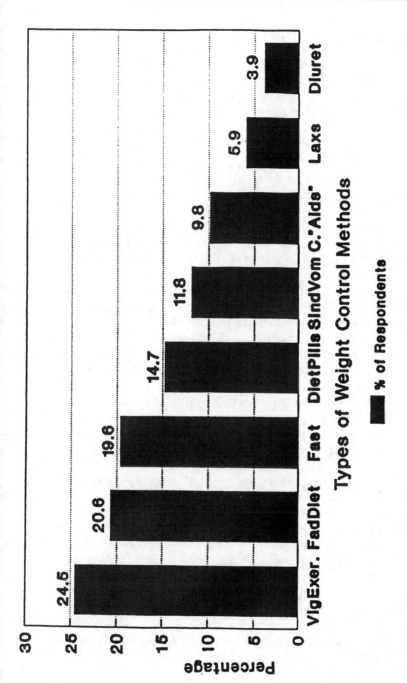

Figure 5.3.   Methods of weight control utilized by female athletes.

included male and female athletes from many sports.) The data from this study also corroborate, and extend to high school athletes, the Burckes-Miller and Black (1988b) suggestion that the prevalence of eating disordered college athletes may exceed the numbers in the general population and that they participate in a wide variety of sports.

The athletes' self-reports in this study unfortunately indicated relatively little communication from their coaches on such important issues as weight loss and dieting. Yet the athletes' concerns about weight were clear. Such concerns are not surprising given the perceived relationship between weight and motor performance. Even so, many of the athletes in this study reported a preoccupation and obsession with weight and food.

It is important to recognize that obsession about food and body image while engaging in potentially harmful practices appears to be, as Orbach (1986) has noted, "a metaphor for our age." The metaphor derives from the following key features: "the starvation amidst plenty, the denial set against desire, [and] the striving for invisibility versus the wish to be seen." This metaphor identifies the psychological underpinnings of a physical and physiologically identified problem.

While this study did not assess personality issues, the observed distorted body images and use of pathogenic weight control methods could certainly be symptomatic of larger psychological issues for some female athletes in this study. Further research to identify the psychological profile that would predispose athletes to eating disorders is necessary.

Many athletes practice poor eating habits yet do not develop eating disorders. However, dieting in adolescence has been identified as a possible precursor to more pathogenic means of weight control (Patton, 1986). Thus, when enough of the predisposing characteristics are present, the drive to improve performance through weight loss may result in an eating disorder.

Whether athletic participation causes eating disorders for those with other predisposing characteristics (as has been suggested by some) cannot be answered by this study. What can and must be addressed, however, is the inflated number of female athletes showing unhealthy weight control practices, body image distortions, and food related problems. It is time to inform and educate all involved about the real dangers that exist for a segment of our athletic population. While weight loss can enhance performance, carried to extremes, it can also result in performance decrement, especially in aerobic activities (Einerson, Ward, & Hanson, 1988). The workshops sponsored by the NCAA are an excellent beginning to the type of education needed.

In summary, this study, along with several others, suggests a trend toward a greater prevalence and pervasiveness of eating disorders among athletes. The progressively larger proportions of eating disordered women in the general population as identified by Crisp, Palmer, & Kalucy (1976), Duddle (1973), Halmi et al. (1981), Mitchell and Eckert (1987), and Orbach (1986) clearly have their analogue in the athletic arena, and the problem may be even more severe (Burckes-Miller & Black, 1988a, 1988b). According to DiBrezzo, Fort, and Ramsdale (1988), the female athletes they assessed recognized the severity of eating related problems. Over half of them felt the need for a professional to speak to them about food restriction, weight loss, and eating disorders.

Sports are supposed to be fun, and the majority of the women in this sample confirmed that as the overriding reason for their participation. Some female athletes, however, cannot be having fun and are perhaps carving out future persistent problems for themselves.

References

Aimez, P. (1983). Violences alimentaires et psychometamorphoses du corps femin. (Alimentary violations and the psychometamorphoses of the female body). *Social Science Information, 22,* 927–940.

Anderson, A. E. (1983). Anorexia and bulimia: A spectrum of eating disorders. *Journal of Adolescent Health Care, 4*(1), 15–21.

Blumenthal, J. A., O'Toole, L. C., & Chang, L. C. (1984). Is running an analogue of anorexia nervosa? *Journal of American Medical Association, 232,* 520–523.

Burckes-Miller, M. E., & Black, D. R. (1988a). Behaviors and attitudes associated with eating disorders: Perceptions of college athletes about food and weight. *Health Education Research, Theory and Practice, 3,* 203–208.

Burckes-Miller, M. E., & Black, D. R. (1988b). Male and female college athletes: Prevalence of anorexia nervosa and bulimia nervosa. *Athletic Training, 23,* 137–140.

Calabrese, L. H. (1985). Nutritional and medical aspects of gymnastics. *Clinical Sports Medicine, 4,* 23–30.

Crisp, A. H., Palmer, R. L., & Kalucy, R. S. (1976). How common is anorexia nervosa? A prevalence study. *British Journal of Psychiatry, 128,* 549–554.

DiBrezzo, R., Fort, E., & Ramsdale, S. (1988). A comparative view of body image and eating disorders in college women athletes versus nonathletes. *Arkansas Journal of Health, Physical Education, Recreation and Dance, 24,* 7–10.

Duddle, M. (1973). An increase of anorexia nervosa in a university population. *British Journal of Psychiatry, 123,* 711–712.

Dummer, G. M., Rosen, L. W., Heusner, W. W., Roberts, P. J., & Counsilman, J. E. (1987). Pathogenic weight-control behaviors of young competitive swimmers. *The Physician and Sportsmedicine, 15*(5), 75–84.

Einerson, J., Ward, A., & Hanson, P. (1988). Exercise responses in females with anorexia nervosa. *International Journal of Eating Disorders, 7*, 253–260.

Epling, W. F., Pierce, W. D., & Stefan, L. (1983). A theory of activity-based anorexia. *International Journal of Eating Disorders, 3*, 27–46.

Falls, H. B., & Humphrey, L. D. (1978). Body type and composition differences between placers and non-placers in an AIAW gymnastics meet. *Research Quarterly, 49*, 38–43.

Friedrichs, M. (1988). The dependent solution: Anorexia and bulimia as defenses against danger. *Women and Therapy, 7*, 53–73.

Halmi, K. A., Falk, K. R., & Schwartz, E. (1981). Binge eating and vomiting: A survey of a college population. *Psychiatric Medicine, 11*, 697–706.

Hand, C. (Producer). (1989). *Afraid to eat: Eating disorders and student athletes.* (Videotape). Wilkes-Barre, PA: Karol Media.

Hesse-Biber, S. (1989). Eating patterns and disorders in a college population: Are women's eating problems a new phenomenon? *Sex Roles, 20*, 71–89.

Katz, J. L. (1986). Long distance running, anorexia nervosa and bulimia: Report of two cases. *Comprehensive Psychiatry, 27*, 74–78.

Knortz, K. A., & Reinhart, R. S. (1984). Women's athletics: The athletic trainer's viewpoint. *Clinical Sports Medicine, 3*, 851–860.

Levenkron, S. L. (1982). *Treating and overcoming anorexia nervosa.* New York: Charles Scribners Sons.

Maloney, M. J. (1983). Anorexia nervosa and bulimia in dancers: Accurate diagnosis and treatment planning. *Clinical Sports Medicine, 2*, 549–555.

Mitchell, J. E., & Eckert, E. D. (1987). Scope and significance of eating disorders. *Journal of Consulting and Clinical Psychology, 55*, 628–634.

Moriarty, D., & Moriarty, M. (1988). Multicultural influences in eating disorders: Introgenesis by health professionals and sport/fitness instructors. Unpublished manuscript.

Orbach, S. (1986). *Hunger strike: The anorectic's struggle as a metaphor for our age.* New York: Avon Books.

Overdorf, V. G. (1990). Eating disorders in the athletic arena. *The Reporter, 63*, 12–13.

Patton, G. C. (1986). The spectrum of eating disorders in adolescence. *Journal of Psychometric Research, 32*, 579–584.

Peters, C., Swassing, G. S., Butterfield, P., & McKay, G. (1984). Assessment and treatment of anorexia nervosa and bulimia in school age children. *School Psychology Review, 13*, 183–191.

Rosen, J. C., & Gross, J. (1987). Prevalence of weight reducing and weight gaining in adolescent girls and boys. *Health Psychology, 6*, 131–147.

Rosen, L. W., McKeag, D. R., Hough, D. O., & Curley, V. (1986). Pathogenic weight-control behavior in female athletes. *The Physician and Sportsmedicine, 14*(1), 79–86.

Short, S. H., & Short, W. R. (1983). Four-year study of university athletes' dietary intake. *Journal of American Dietetic Association, 82,* 632–645.

Steiner-Adair, C. (1988–89). Developing the voice of the wise woman: College students and bulimia. *Journal of College Student Psychotherapy, 3,* 151–165.

Szmukler, G. I., Eisler, I., Gillies, C., & Hayward, M. E. (1985). The implications of anorexia nervosa in a ballet school. *Journal of Psychiatric Research, 19,* 177–181.

Yager, J. (1988). The treatment of eating disorders. *Journal of Clinical Psychiatry, 49,* 18–25.

Author Notes

The author expresses appreciation for the excellent editing and insightful conceptual comments provided by David R. Black; his guidance and attention to detail shaped this paper into its present form. Beth E. Barnett is also thanked for her reading of the final draft, and Beva Eastman for preparation of the tables. Finally, acknowledgement is given to two wonderful athletes, Pam and Nancy, who shaped my interest in this field.

APPENDIX 5.A

Survey of Eating Patterns of Athletes
(Adapted from Eating Habits of Athletes Survey
developed by Burckes-Miller & Black, 1988a, 1988b
Modified by V.G. Overdorf)

Last four numbers of social security _____

Instructions.
  This survey is requesting information about your eating habits and athletic experience. Answer honestly; there are no right or wrong answers.
Since you do not put your name on this survey, your answers are confidential. You are to circle the letter of the correct answer (and in some cases
you may get to circle more than one answer). Thank you very much for
your assistance in taking this survey.

  1. What year in school are you presently?

     A. Fr—HS   E. Fr—College
     B. Soph—HS   F. Soph—Coll
     C. Jr—HS   G. Jr—Coll
     D. Sr—HS   H. Sr—Coll
                                I. Other _____

  2. Sex

     A. Female   B. Male

  3. What is your height?

     _____ ft., _____ in.

  4. What is your weight?

     _____

  5. On what team are you presently competing?

     A. Cross Country   H. Softball/Baseball
     B. Track   I. Gymnastics
     C. Field Hockey   J. Soccer
     D. Volleyball   K. Fencing
     E. Tennis   L. Bowling
     F. Swimming   M. Wrestling
     G. Basketball   N. Dance
                                O. Other _____

  6. How long have you been competing in this sport?

     A. 1 yr   E. 5 yrs
     B. 2 yrs   F. 6 yrs
     C. 3 yrs   G. 7 yrs
     D. 4 yrs   H. 8 yrs
                                I. Other _____

7. How would you characterize your ability in this sport?

   A. Beginner
   B. Advanced beginner
   C. Intermediate
   D. Advanced
   E. "Elite" athlete (Olympic level, national level, etc.)

8. How would you characterize your training habits for the sport you are presently competing in? (More than one answer may be circled)

   A. Only practice during regularly scheduled practices
   B. Do a little extra training outside of practice
   C. Do excessive training outside of practice
   D. Do an "off-season" program to prepare for competition
   E. Whether in season or out of season, I overtrain excessively

9. Has your coach ever talked to your team about how important it is to lose weight to improve overall performance?

   A. Never
   B. "Sort of" mentioned it casually
   C. Talks about it frequently
   D. Stresses it constantly

10. Has your coach ever told *you* specifically that you need to lose weight to improve your performance?

   A. Never   C. Several times
   B. Once   D. Stresses it constantly

(If you answered D, describe your feelings about the comments _____

_____

_____

11. Do you feel that you would be able to remain on this team if you did not maintain a particular weight?

   A. Yes   B. No   C. Has no bearing

12. What reason(s) best describes why you participate on this team? (You may circle more than one)

   A. Recognition   F. Helps control my weight
   B. Self-esteem   G. Parental pressure
   C. Fun   H. Peer pressure
   D. Socialization   I. Coaches' pressure
   E. Gives me confidence   J. Other _____

Continued on next page

13. Have you ever used any of the following methods for weight loss? (More than one answer may be circled)

   A. Fad diet
   B. Diuretics (water pills)
   C. Laxatives
   D. Self-induced vomiting
   E. Fasting (eating no food for 24 hours or more)
   F. Excessive or constant vigorous exercise
   G. Enemas
   H. Diet pills
   I. Commercially bought "aids" to curb your appetite

14. Over the past year, what has been the greatest fluctuation in weight that you have experienced at one time?

   A. 0–3 lbs   D. 10–12 lbs
   B. 4–6 lbs   E. 12–14 lbs
   C. 7–9 lbs   F. 15+ lbs

15. How would you characterize yourself in regard to thoughts about your weight?

   A. I hardly ever think about it
   B. I think about it sometimes
   C. I think about it quite a lot
   D. I think about it all the time
   E. I can never get it off my mind and that concerns me

16. Have you ever received professional counseling (e.g., from a psychologist, psychiatrist, etc.) regarding an abusive treatment of food?

   A. Never   D. On a regular basis
   B. Once   E. Think I should but have been afraid
   C. Several times   to

17. Have you ever eaten a great amount of food and then self-induced vomiting?

   A. Never   C. Often
   B. Once   D. Very frequently

18. How would you characterize your weight?

   A. Just right   D. A little too thin
   B. Much too heavy   E. Much too thin
   C. A little too heavy

19. How do most others characterize your weight?

   A. Just right   D. A little too thin
   B. Much too heavy   E. Much too thin
   C. A little too heavy

20. Does your coach monitor your weight?

    A. Never   C. Frequently
    B. Sometimes   D. Almost daily

21. Which of the following refer to you? (You may answer more than one)

    A. I don't like to eat when other people are present
    B. I often am depressed after I eat
    C. I dread mealtime
    D. People in authority positions force me to eat, even tho' I don't want to
    E. I have missed at least three consecutive menstrual cycles that should have occurred (females only)

22. Have you ever been diagnosed with an eating disorder?

    A. No   C. Yes, bulimia nervosa
    B. Yes, anorexia nervosa   D. Yes, both anorexia and bulimia

23. Do *you* think you might have an eating disorder?

    A. Yes   B. No

24. How often do you eat small quantities of food (600 calories a day or less) as a means of weight control?

    A. Never
    B. Rarely—1 day per month
    C. 2–3 days per month
    D. 1 day a week
    E. 2 or more days per week

25. I have an intense fear of becoming obese even though I am under weight or normal weight right now.

    A. Yes   B. No

6

Do Female College Athletes Develop Eating Disorders as a Result of the Athletic Environment?

JOANNE S. CHOPAK

MARY TAYLOR-NICHOLSON

The purpose of this study was to investigate whether female athletes develop eating disorders as a result of factors in the athletic environment. A questionnaire containing the Eating Disorder Inventory (EDI) and a Survey of Eating Disorders Among Athletes (SEDA) was administered to 100 female college athletes from six varsity teams during the spring of 1987. Significant differences were found between the gymnastics team and the basketball and lacrosse teams. The response rate was 79% and 24 (30%) athletes indicated they had an eating disorder at some time in their lives. Of the 24, 16 (66%) thought their eating disorder became more of a problem as a result of their participation in sports. The study offers suggestions as to what health professionals can do to increase awareness of eating disorders among athletes.

The prevalence of eating disorders, specifically anorexia nervosa and bulimia nervosa, in college student populations has been well publicized in recent years (Burckes-Miller & Black, 1988; Drewnowski, Hopkins, & Kessler, 1988; Pope, Hudson, Yurgelun-Todd, & Hudson, 1984; Schotte & Stunkard, 1987; Zuckerman, Colby, Ware, & Lazerson, 1986). Whether this increase in publicity has led to a greater awareness in the smaller subpopulation of college coaches and athletes remains to be seen. Some researchers have suggested that the incidence of eating disorders is higher among athletes because the athletic environment focuses on body form and weight (Zucker et al., 1985; Borgen & Corbin, 1987).

Literature focusing on eating disorder behaviors among athletes began appearing in the early 1980s (Buikel, 1983; Combs, 1982; Costar, 1983). Many of these studies focused on sports that emphasized leanness and body size. Costar (1983), in his survey of 41 female gymnasts, found that 24% of them had used self-induced vomiting and/or laxatives to control their weight. Rosen, McKeag, Hough, and Curley (1986) studied 182 female college athletes competing in 10 different sports. They examined the types of methods athletes used to control their weight. Of the athletes surveyed, 32% reported practicing some type of unhealthy weight control behavior (e.g., self-induced vomiting, abuse of diet pills, and/or use of diuretics). Borgen and Corbin (1987) compared athletes whose sport or artistic discipline emphasized leanness (gymnastics, cheerleading, ballet dancing, body building/weight training) with athletes whose sports did not have this focus (swimming, track and field, volleyball). Using the Eating Disorder Inventory (EDI), they found 20% of the athletes in the group whose sports emphasized leanness were either preoccupied with their weight or demonstrated eating disorder tendencies, compared with 10% of the athletes in the group whose sports did not emphasize leanness.

The purpose of this study was to investigate whether athletes develop eating disorders from factors within the athletic environment (e.g., weight loss being required to achieve an aesthetic ideal of beauty for participation).

Method

Subjects

Subjects were members of the women's basketball, diving, gymnastics, lacrosse, swimming, and tennis teams from a large northeastern university. Of the 100 team members who received questionnaires, 79 responded for a 79% response rate. Thirty-one of the athletes (39%) were freshmen, 27 (34%) were sophomores, and the remaining 21 (27%) were almost equally divided between juniors and seniors. Seventy-four athletes (94%) were Caucasian and five (6%) were Afro-American. The average height of the sample was 65.8 in. and the average weight was 135.8 lb. Twenty-two athletes (28%) were on a full athletic scholarship, 24 (30%) were on a partial scholarship, and 33 (42%) were not receiving any scholarship money.

Procedure

Questionnaire Administration. Questionnaires were administered to female college athletes participating in varsity sports at a large north-eastern university during the spring of 1987. The study was limited to sports whose competitive season was during the second half of the school year. The research questionnaire consisted of two instruments: the "Eating Disorder Inventory" (EDI) (Garner, Olmsted, & Polivy, 1984) and the "Survey of Eating Disorders Among Athletes" (SEDA) (Guthrie, 1985). The EDI is a 64-item self-report instrument used to measure psychological and behavioral traits related to anorexia nervosa and bulimia. For scoring purposes the EDI is divided into eight sub-scales (as listed in Table 6.2). Reliability for EDI was reported for each subscale. The final average item-total correlation was .63 (Garner, Olmsted, & Polivy, 1983). The EDI was validated after determining that it sufficiently differentiated between the two original sample populations (clinical anorexics and females from a college comparision group) (Garner et al., 1983). The EDI is not recommended as a diagnostic instrument and therefore ideal for nonclinical settings. Furthermore, its reliability and validity have been documented numerous times in studies in which it has been used (Borgen & Corbin, 1987; Garner et al., 1983; Guthrie, 1985; Kurtzman, Yager, Landsverk, Wiesmeier, & Bodurka, 1989; Zuckerman, et al., 1986).

The SEDA[1] is a 33-item survey that asks respondents to identify whether they have ever had an eating disorder (anorexia nervosa, bulimia, binge eating), and if so, at what age, and whether they believed participation in athletics contributed to the onset of their eating disorder. Content validity was established using a panel of experts in the field of eating disorders. The panel consisted of counseling and clinical psychologists, sport psychologists, and physical educators who worked with athletes who had eating disorders. A high degree of content validity was established. Similar to the EDI, for analyzing purposes the survey was divided into three categories. High reliability was reported for all but one category (the questions asking about external pressures and their contribution to the development of eating disorders), with a Cronbach's alpha of .50 (external pressures), .90 (athletic environment), and .73 (preventive measures). Definitions for anorexia nervosa-restrictive type, anorexia nervosa-bulimic type, bulimia, and binge eating were provided in the SEDA section of the questionnaire. A mean score for each team by category was calculated. On the SEDA, a high mean score indicates levels of agreement, contribution, and helpfulness as indicated

---

[1]This questionnaire was used with permission of the author.

by the respondents. A demographic section was also included in the questionnaire and contained questions on weight perception, weight satisfaction, class standing, scholarship status, level of team participation (first, second, and third string), and ethnic background.

Data Collection and Analysis

The coaches of the teams chosen to participate were initially contacted by mail by the investigators. A follow-up phone call was made to each coach one week after mailing to obtain permission to administer the survey and to determine a convenient time and location to do so. In most cases, the most convenient time chosen to distribute the surveys was before practice. In cases where the researchers were unable to administer the survey in person, the coaches of the teams were given specific instructions. This occurred in half the cases. At the beginning of the survey session, the researchers explained to the athletes that the survey was anonymous and participation was strictly voluntary.

Frequencies and analysis of variance were employed for analyzing the data. Mean scores were calculated for each team individually as well as for the entire sample.

Results

SEDA

Twenty-four athletes (30%) reported having an eating disorder either currently or in the past. Twelve athletes (15%) who identified themselves as having a history of eating disorders believed they still had an eating disorder at the time the survey was completed.

Of the 24 athletes who reported having had an eating disorder, 16 (20%) indicated their eating disorder began in high school, while 6 (8%) specified college and 2 (3%) noted junior high school. All 24 athletes participated in sports when their eating disorder began. Additionally, 16 (20%) athletes thought their eating disorder became more problematic as a result of participation in sports.

Table 6.1 shows the results of the SEDA for each team for 20 of the 24 athletes reporting a past or present eating disorder.

The gymnasts, who had a higher team mean score in all three areas than any other group, reported that pressure to maintain aesthetic beauty ideals made a strong contribution to the onset of their problem.

Table 6.1

Summary Results of Survey of Eating Disorders Among Athletes (SEDA) for Eating Disordered Athletes

Team	(n)	External Pressures		Athletic Environment		Preventive Measures	
		M	SD	M	SD	M	SD
Basketball	3	0.0	0.0	10.0	1.7	21.0	4.1
Diving	4	15.0	0.0	13.8	1.9	20.0	1.4
Gymnastics	5	16.3	.57	16.6	1.8	19.5	5.8
Lacrosse	2	11.5	.7	8.5	.7	20.7	3.7
Swimming	5	15.8	2.4	12.6	3.4	22.3	4.0
Tennis	1	14.0	0.0	15.0	0.0	20.2	5.6

Other environmental influences the gymnasts thought might have contributed to their eating disorder were being required to lose weight to achieve high performance levels and a remark made by a coach or athletic trainer regarding their weight.

EDI

The results from the Eating Disorders Inventory are presented in Table 6.2. On the Drive for Thinness subscale, an analysis of variance indicated a significant difference, $F(5,73) = 4.25$, $p < .01$. There was also a significant difference between the gymnastics and lacrosse teams as indicated by multiple range test Scheffé, $(5,73) = 4.84$, $p < .05$. These results were consistent with those found in the SEDA, suggesting the strong emphasis on low body weight that is characteristic of the sport of gymnastics (Rosen & Hough, 1988).

Discussion

The results suggest that factors in the athletic environment contribute to eating disorders or, at the very least, maladaptive eating behaviors are a reality among female athletes. Athletes participating in sports which emphasize leanness (gymnastics, diving, and swimming) reported a higher frequency of an eating disorder history than the athletes in the three other sports studied (basketball, lacrosse, and tennis). This is very similar to the finding of Borgen and Corbin (1987). They reported 20% of the athletes who participated in gymnastics, ballet, and cheer-

Table 6.2

Eating Disorder Inventory (EDI) of Athletes by Sport and Subscale

EDI Subscale (N=79)	F value	Mean Score (all teams)	Basketball (n=10)		Diving (n=5)		Gymnastics (n=12)		Lacrosse (n=29)		Swimming (n=17)		Tennis (n=6)	
			MD	SD	M	SD	M	SD	M	SD	M	SD	M	SD
1. Drive for Thinness[a]	4.25	5.5	2.4	3.6	9.4	1.1	9.5	7.8	3.3	4.6	7.1	5.1	4.7	4.8
2. Bulimia	3.28	1.2	.5	1.0	1.0	1.7	2.8	2.9	.6	1.0	1.8	2.4	.2	.4
3. Body Dissatisfaction	2.34	9.9	4.7	3.9	8.4	3.4	13.7	8.3	8.8	6.9	12.1	7.3	10.5	8.8
4. Ineffectiveness	3.37	1.4	.9	1.3	.2	.4	1.6	2.2	.8	1.6	3.3	3.6	.2	.4
5. Perfectionism	1.28	6.4	8.8	5.2	4.4	2.3	7.7	4.2	6.0	4.3	5.8	3.1	5.3	5.5
6. Interpersonal Distrust	.61	2.0	1.4	1.9	1.3	1.5	2.7	2.1	2.4	2.9	1.9	2.0	1.2	2.9
7. Interoceptive Awareness	.84	2.3	1.7	2.2	2.4	1.1	3.8	4.0	1.9	2.5	2.1	2.9	2.0	2.9
8. Maturity Fears	.51	2.1	2.1	1.1	2.0	1.6	1.6	1.4	1.9	1.6	2.6	1.9	2.1	1.6

[a]At the $p < .05$ level, a post hoc Scheffé test showed gymnastics differed significantly from the lacrosse team.

leading were preoccupied with their weight or had tendencies toward eating disorders. A recommendation for future research would be to include cheerleaders or university pom-pon squads as athletes who might be at risk for developing an eating disorder.

Environmental factors such as pressure from coaches or teammates to lose weight for the aesthetic beauty of their sport was identified by many of the respondents, but significantly by the gymnastics team, as contributing to the development of their eating disorder. The coach or athletic trainer seems to play a significant role in an athlete's life. What they eat and with whom they eat may all be influenced by the coach. In two cases the researchers were not present to administer the survey. Therefore, there is the potential for response bias and the possibility that the number of eating disorders or abnormal eating behaviors is even higher than was reported. Additionally, competition between teammates may also be a potential factor affecting the athletes and the onset of an eating disorder. Being required to lose or maintain a specific weight to achieve high performance levels or a certain aesthetic ideal (and possibly not to lose their spot to another team member) was reported as making a strong contribution to the onset of eating disorders among the gymnasts.

The strong suggestion of environmental influence (i.e., from coach or teammates) has been reported by other researchers (Costar, 1983; Rosen et al., 1986; Rosen & Hough, 1988). They report that female gymnasts may be more susceptible to the development of an eating disorder as a result of comments regarding their weight, as well as perceived aesthetic ideals that are associated with the sport (Costar, 1983; Rosen et al., 1986; Rosen & Hough, 1988). Therefore, it is essential that health and physical educators and coaches develop a better understanding and a greater sensitivity to the environmental risk factors associated with eating disorders and abnormal eating behaviors among athletes. With 24 (30%) of the 79 female athletes reporting an eating disorder, the development of educational programs for athletes would seem clearly mandated. Because most female athletes reported that their eating problems began to some degree in high school, further study of athletes at the secondary school level is also suggested.

Furthermore, Combs (1982) suggests that teachers, coaches, and parents of female athletes not overemphasize leanness. In addition, she recommends that coaches and parents not demand specific amounts of weight loss for an athlete without considering the athlete's specific body composition. Overdorf (1987) suggests that coaches rethink their strategies for encouraging athletes to "get in shape," so that getting into shape does not lead to excessive dieting. She also believes that winning should be deemphasized or at least kept in perspective, so performance expectations are realistic. The results of this study should be of value to health educators, coaches, and other health personnel who play a significant role in an athlete's life. Clearly, the influence of the athletic environment that may lead to an eating disorder among female athletes appears to be serious enough to warrant intervention.

References

Borgen, J. S., & Corbin, C. B. (1987). Eating disorders among female athletes. *The Physician and Sportsmedicine, 15*(2), 89–95.

Buikel, S. (1983). Anorexia nervosa and bulimia in athletics. *Athletic Training, 18*, 137–138.

Burckes-Miller, M. E., & Black, D. R. (1988). Male and female college athletes: Prevalence of anorexia nervosa and bulimia nervosa. *Athletic Training, 23*, 137–140.

Combs, M. R. (1982). By food possessed. *Women's Sports, 4*(2), 12–17.

Costar, E. D. (1983). Gymnasts at risk. *International Gymnast, 25*, 58–59.

Drewnowski, A., Hopkins, S. A., & Kessler, R. C. (1988). The prevalence of bulimia nervosa in the U.S. college student population. *American Journal of Public Health, 78*, 1322–1324.

Garner, D. M., Olmsted, M. P., & Polivy, J. (1983). Development and validation of a multidimensional eating disorder inventory for anorexia and bulimia. *International Journal of Eating Disorders, 2*, 15–34.

Garner, D. M., Olmsted, M. P., & Polivy, J. (1984). *Manual for eating disorder inventory (EDI)*. Odessa, FL: Psychological Assessment Resources, Inc.

Guthrie, S. R. (1985). The prevalence and development of eating disorders within a selected intercollegiate population. *Dissertation Abstracts International, 46*, 12A. (University Microfilms No. 8603006).

Kurtzman, F. D., Yager, J., Landsverk, J., Wiesmeier, E., & Bodurka, D. C. (1989). Eating disorders among selected female student populations at UCLA. *Journal of the American Dietetic Association, 89*, 45–53.

Overdorf, V. G. (1987). Conditioning for thinness: The dilemma of eating-disordered female athletes. *Journal of Physical Education, Recreation and Dance, 58*(4), 62–64.

Pope, H. G., Hudson, J. I., Yurgelun-Todd, D., & Hudson, M. S. (1984). Prevalence of anorexia nervosa and bulimia in three student populations. *International Journal of Eating Disorders, 3*, 45–51.

Rosen, L. W., & Hough, D. O. (1988). Pathogenic weight-control behaviors of female college gymnasts. *The Physician and Sportsmedicine, 16*(9), 141–146.

Rosen, L. W., McKeag, D. B., Hough, D. O., & Curley, V. (1986). Pathogenic weight control behavior in female athletes. *The Physician and Sportsmedicine, 14*(1), 79–86.

Schotte, D. E., & Stunkard, A. J. (1987). Bulimia vs. bulimic behaviors on a college campus. *Journal of the American Medical Association, 258,* 1213–1215.

Zucker, P., Avener, J., Bayder, S., Boatman, A., Moore, L., & Zimmerman, J. (1985). Eating disorders in young athletes. *The Physician and Sportsmedicine, 13*(11), 88–106.

Zuckerman, D. M., Colby, A., Ware, N. C., & Lazerson, J. S. (1986). The prevalence of bulimia among college students. *American Journal of Public Health, 76,* 1135–1137.

Author Notes

The authors wish to express their sincere gratitude to David R. Black and Judy Black for their diligent assistance with the revision of this manuscript.

7

Weight Control Among Elite Women Swimmers

ROSEANN BENSON

The female swimmers at the 1988 United States Olympic Selection Meet (N=394) responded to a questionnaire about psychological and behavioral characteristics related to eating disorders. A multiple response item indicated that these women had used many methods to lose weight, including meal skipping (81.9%), steam or sauna baths (21.9%), fasting for 24 hours or longer (14.8%), self-induced vomiting (14.4%), a protein diet substitute (12.9%), non-prescription appetite suppressants (12.5%), and laxatives (10.8%). Almost 70% of the swimmers reported that coaches told them to lose weight; 41% believed they needed to lose weight to swim faster; 50% believed they needed to lose to look better; and 36% reported that pressure to lose weight was detrimental to helping them meet performance goals. Some were angry and resentful about restrictions or punishment for not achieving a particular weight. Recommendations are made for educating swimmers and coaches that emphasize refocusing on realistic goals of body fat and a healthy lifestyle rather than weight.

The *ideal* female in the American culture is one who is sleek, slender, and thin. Erroneously, these women are thought to be lean, fit, and healthy. While the terms *sleek, slender,* and *thin* describe a look, they do not describe the quality of the look. On the other hand, terms like *lean* and *fit* connote health. They include the concepts of lean-to-fat tissue ratio. For elite female athletes (national and international competitors), the subtle nuances separating the meanings of these groups of words can spell the difference between success and failure. The failure of these athletes—and their coaches and families—to understand the application of the concept of lean-to-fat tissue ratio can lead to unrealistic criteria for weight management.

Generally, athletes demonstrate more tendencies toward eating disorder behaviors if appearance is important to outcome, the competitive

97

uniform exposes much of the body, the skill is performed in the air, and individual performance is emphasized rather than team performance (Combs, 1982). However, research studies of female athletes have reported ineffective, unhealthy, and potentially dangerous weight loss techniques used by participants in a variety of sports, not all of which fit the above criteria (Black & Burckes-Miller, 1988). Tendencies for eating disorders have been found among female athletes participating in basketball, cheerleading, field hockey, golf, gymnastics, softball, swimming, tennis, track and field, and volleyball (Borgen & Corbin, 1987; Burckes-Miller & Black, 1988; Clark, Nelson, & Evans, 1988; Dummer, Rosen, Heusner, Roberts, & Counsilman, 1987; Lundholm & Littrell, 1986; Rosen & Hough, 1988; Rosen, McKeag, Hough, & Curley, 1986). Only Dummer et al. (1987) reported swimmers to be at risk.

The purposes of this study were to investigate a larger number of swimmers to determine if prior trends were upheld and if tendencies toward eating disorder behaviors were observed among elite women swimmers. Specifically, the study was conducted to identify the perceptions of elite women swimmers about the importance of weight and to assess psychological and behavioral characteristics in regard to eating disorders.

Method

Subjects

The population consisted of United States collegiate, high school, and United States Swimming club competitive swimmers. To be eligible to compete in the United States Olympic Selection Meet, swimmers (U.S. citizenship) had to meet a time standard between January 1, 1987 and August 3, 1988 at a meet officially sanctioned by United States Swimming or the National Collegiate Athletic Association. An official verification card or proof of performance, signed by a meet official representing the respective organization, was required to corroborate the time.

There were 410 women who met the criteria and could be included in the study. Of those eligible, 15 were eliminated because follow-up postcards and questionnaires were returned stamped "incorrect address" or "no forwarding address available" by the post office. Additionally, one participant was disqualified from the meet because she did not pass the drug test. Of the 394 swimmers who could be contacted, 75.6% chose to participate.

Respondents averaged 18.6 years old (14 to 30 years), 5 foot 8 inches tall (62 to 74 in.), 136 lb (90 to 180 lb), 16.2% body fat (5% to 25%), and 10.8 years of competitive swimming (3 to 25 years). They also averaged between their freshman and sophomore years of college (grade 8 to postbaccalaureate).

Procedures

Questionnaire Development. The Eating Disorder Inventory (EDI), developed by Garner, Olmsted, and Polivy (1983), was used to assess the athletes. It has been shown to be a reliable and valid instrument used to screen for tendencies toward eating disorders (Raciti & Norcross, 1987).

The EDI consists of eight subscales which measure characteristics associated with anorexia and bulimia. The Drive for Thinness subscale indicates an obsessive concern with dieting and an extreme preoccupation with weight and thinness. The extreme pursuit of thinness is a feature of anorexia nervosa and reflects both a desire to lose weight and a fear of gaining weight. The Bulimia subscale indicates tendencies for bingeing, which may be followed by self-induced vomiting. The Body Dissatisfaction subscale measures the perception that certain body parts are too large. The Perfectionism subscale measures excessive personal expectations for superior achievement. The Interpersonal Distrust subscale measures lack of self-assurance in recognizing and identifying emotions as well as sensations of hunger or satiety. The Interoceptive Awareness subscale assesses low self-efficacy in recognizing and accurately identifying emotions and/or visceral sensations of hunger or satiety. The Maturity Fears subscale measures desire to retreat to the security of preadolescence due to fears of adulthood. The Ineffectiveness subscale assesses feeling of inadequacy, insecurity, worthlessness, and perceptions about the degree of control individuals have over their lives.

Additional questions were developed to address perceived nutritional awareness, weight control techniques, beliefs about weight, perceived pressure to conform to a particular weight or percent body fat, and demographic information. Validity was examined by a panel of nine experts reviewing the questionnaire (Windsor, Baranowski, Clark, & Cutter, 1984). The panel consisted of a registered nurse, a registered dietician, a medical doctor, a doctor of public health, two health educators, a former elite swimmer, and two elite swimming coaches.

The final form of the questionnaire (including the EDI) consisted of 128 questions; 121 were close-ended with Likert-type, dichotomous or checklist response format and 7 questions were open-ended of which 4 required in-depth responses.

A pilot study was conducted to determine reliability of the complete instrument. Stability, established through test-retest comparison after two weeks, was estimated at .68. Internal consistency, established through Cronbach alpha, was estimated at .91.

Questionnaire Administration. The questionnaire titled *Selected Eating Practices and Weight Control Techniques Among Elite Women Swimmers* was mailed or delivered to all 410 female swimmers at the 1988 U.S. Olympic Selection Meet.

Research Variables. The PRECEDE framework (Green, Kreuter, Deeds, & Partridge, 1980) was selected as a theoretical base for developing the variables. The general variable categories selected for this study included Predisposing Factors, Enabling Factors, Reinforcing Factors, and Behavioral Factors, which are associated with the Health Problem (eating disorders).

Research Design. An ex-post facto cross-sectional research design was selected. A descriptive method was chosen to meet the primary objective of establishing baseline data on the prevalence of unhealthy eating patterns and weight control techniques among elite women swimmers. This was performed by examining psychological and behavioral tendencies toward eating disorders.

Data Analyses. The closed-answer data were analyzed using SAS® statistical package subroutines for frequency and central tendency. Open-ended responses were subjected to a modified content analysis for categorization.

Results

Weight Control Methods

The primary methods reported by elite women swimmers for controlling weight were meal skipping and exercise outside of swimming practice (see Table 7.1). Additional methods of weight control included sauna or steam room, fasting, self-induced vomiting, liquid protein diet drink, nonprescription appetite suppressants, laxatives, nonbreathing plastic "sauna suits," diuretics, and prescription appetite suppressants. The total reported in Table 7.1 is greater than 100% because many respondents used more than one technique.

Table 7.1

**Weight Control Methods of Elite Women Swimmers
(expressed in percentages)**
$N = 298$

Variable	N	R	S	O	U	A
Additional Exercise	12.1	19.5	29.3	17.8	14.5	6.7
Skipped Meals	18.1	30.2	30.5	15.1	4.7	1.3
Sauna or Steam Room	78.1	13.8	5.4	2.0	0.3	0.3
Fasting for 24 Hours or Longer	85.2	8.8	4.7	1.3	0.0	0.0
Self-induced Vomiting	85.6	7.0	4.7	1.3	0.7	0.7
Protein Diet Substitute	87.1	9.5	1.4	1.4	0.7	0.0
Nonprescription Appetite Suppressants	87.5	8.8	3.1	0.3	0.3	0.0
Laxatives	89.2	5.7	3.4	1.0	0.7	0.7
Sauna Suit	94.3	2.7	2.4	0.3	0.3	0.0
Diuretics	95.3	2.4	1.0	0.7	0.7	0.0
Prescription Appetite Suppressants	97.3	1.7	0.7	0.3	0.0	0.0

Note. N = never, R = rarely, S = sometimes, O = often, U = usually, A = always

The subjects also reported binge eating. Binge eating, however, is a relative term for each individual, and consequently, a conservative approach to collapsing the columns was taken. By combining the "often," "usually," and "always" responses in Table 7.2, almost 22% of the women ate when upset. Combining all the responses except "never," 57.4% had thought at sometime about bingeing, 54.4% reported they ate normally in groups but binged alone, 49.8% reported uncontrollable eating binges, and 45% reported they had considered using self-induced vomiting for weight control.

Swim Team Program

A summary of the role of the swim team program in providing nutrition and weight control education, weight or percent body fat measurement, and direction to lose weight is contained in Table 7.3. Columns "rarely," "sometimes," "often," "usually," and "always" are collapsed on these items. As shown in Table 7.3, 65.5% and 56.7%, respectively, of the elite women swimmers reported "sometimes," "rarely," or "never" was nutrition or weight control education an integral part of their swim team program. Although almost 60% reported their weight was regularly ("often," "usually," "always") measured at swimming practice, less than 33% reported their percent body fat was regularly measured ("seldom," "rarely" or "never") measured at swimming

Table 7.2
Bulimic Tendencies of Elite Women Swimmers
(expressed in percentages)
N = 298

Variable	N	R	S	O	U	A
Stuff Self with Food	7.4	36.7	39.4	12.5	3.7	0.3
Eat when Upset	10.4	28.6	39.1	11.4	8.1	2.4
Think about Bingeing	42.6	33.1	13.2	5.4	5.1	0.7
Eat Normally in Groups, Binge Alone	45.6	29.4	16.2	5.1	2.7	1.0
Uncontrollable Eating Binges	50.2	26.3	15.8	6.4	0.3	1.0
Have Thought of Self-induced Vomiting to Lose Weight	55.1	21.3	14.9	6.4	2.4	0.0

Note. N = never, R = rarely, S = sometimes, O = often, U = usually, A = always

Table 7.3
Role of Coaches/Others in Weight Control of Elite Women Swimmers
(expressed in percentages)
N = 298

Variable	N	R	S	O	U	A
Nutrition Education	13.8	27.2	24.5	13.1	14.1	7.4
Weight Control Education	14.1	22.8	19.8	13.8	13.1	17.1
Weight Measured	15.2	11.8	13.5	9.5	18.9	31.1
% Fat Measured	22.5	19.1	26.2	7.0	12.1	13.1
Told to Lose Weight						
By Coach	30.5	22.5	27.5	3.7	5.0	10.7
By Parents	63.1	19.5	9.7	2.7	3.4	1.7
By Physician	92.3	6.1	1.7	0.0	0.0	0.0

Note. N = never, R = rarely, S = sometimes, O = often, U = usually, A = always

practice. Yet, almost 70% of these elite athletes reported their coaches at some time ("rarely," "sometimes," "often," "usually," and "always") had told them to lose weight.

The best competitive swim weight for elite women swimmers was determined most often by the swimmer herself (53%), followed by her coach (36%), or the two individuals combined (8.8%). The two top methods reported by elite women swimmers for determining best competitive swimming weight were weighing (27.5%) and subjective "feel" (20%).

Responses to questions concerning pressure to lose weight revealed that 36% reported this effort was detrimental to helping them meet performance goals. Responses to open-ended questions revealed intense anger and resentment for punitive restrictions or punishment for not making a particular weight.

Great differences in sensitivity were observed in the open-ended responses by elite women swimmers concerning their feelings about weight and percent body fat being made public and about restrictions for not making certain weights. Some were very sensitive about their weight and percent body fat and did not want either of these statistics made public to their teammates. Some swimmers reported being restricted for not maintaining a certain weight. Most of those who were given additional exercise, specifically not swimming, felt the addition was positive. Those who were restricted in punitive ways (e.g., not permitted to travel, not permitted to swim with the team, not allowed snacks, not allowed to eat, or "kicked off" the team) generally were very negative in their response to the restriction. Some reported that these restrictions led to feelings of discouragement, worthlessness, depression, and loss of self-esteem.

Importance of Low Weight

Low weight was reported by the elite women swimmers in this study to be important, not only to swim faster, but also to look better (see Table 7.4). More swimmers reported interest in weight loss in order to look better (50%) rather than to swim faster (41%). Additionally, they were more convinced that weight rather than the ratio of lean to fat tissue was important for swimming fast (84.2% compared to 72.2%).

Almost 43% of the elite women swimmers in this study reported being on some type of diet to lose weight at the time of the Olympic Selection Meet. Open-ended responses reflected their perceptions of the harmful effects of obsession with weight, yet nearly 42% of the elite women swimmers in this study weighed daily or more often.

The Drive for Thinness subscale (combining "often," "usually," and "always"), shown in Table 7.5, demonstrated that 59.1% were concerned about dieting, 38.2% described themselves as preoccupied with a desire to be thinner, and 51.7% stated they were terrified of gaining weight. However, 32.3% reported they exaggerated the importance of weight.

Discussion

The profile of the elite women swimmers in this study closely resembles that of elite female swimmers reported by Troup et al. (1986) and Sharp (1985). Sharp, in examining a group of elite women swimmers, reported a percent body fat computed from skinfolds of 17.4%. In this study, the self-reported body fat average was 16.2% ($SD = 3.35$), with a minimum of 5% and a maximum of 25%. Twenty individuals in this study reported percent body fat ranging from 5% to 14%. Based on other studies (Fleck, 1983) in which skinfold measurements were used, the low percentages reported by the elite women swimmers may be inaccurate. This possible inaccuracy could be due to the variety of methods used in measurement (underwater weighing, skinfold calipers, and bioelectrical impedance), varying abilities of the individuals doing the measuring, the variability in the accuracy of the instruments themselves, variability in the formulas used to calculate percent body fat, as well as incorrect reporting.

In order to control weight, some athletes in this study used ineffective, unhealthy, and potentially life-threatening methods to lose weight, including dehydration techniques, fasting, self-induced vomiting, and use of appetite suppressants or laxatives. Other methods such as meal skipping and additional exercise, although probably not dangerous, may not be healthy if they promote rapid weight loss. It appears that these swimmers did not know the dangers of certain techniques or that rapid weight loss was more important to them than health. Some of the women may be reinforced to use unhealthy techniques because they were successful in reaching a high level of swimming proficiency. Even though three out of four elite women swimmers reported that they were not using any type of potentially dangerous weight control techniques, Rosen and Hough (1988) stated that the use of these techniques may be underreported.

As noted in the Bulimia subscale results, a significant number of elite women swimmers reported uncontrollable binges. Incidences of occasional overeating are possibly not very different from the general

Table 7.4

Beliefs About Importance of Low Weight Among Elite Women Swimmers
(expressed in percentages)
N = 298

Variable	SD/ D	N	A/ SA
Weight Loss Required for Performance Excellence	19.6	32.3	48.1
Thinner Swimmers Swim Faster	20.8	24.2	55.0
I Could Swim Faster If I Lost Weight	31.9	21.8	46.3
Need to Be at Optimal Weight for Best Performance	3.7	12.1	84.2
Need to Be at Optimal % Fat for Best Performance	5.0	22.8	72.2
Pressure to Lose Weight Helps	60.7	20.1	19.2
Pressure to Lose Weight Is Detrimental	40.3	23.5	36.2
I Need to Lose Weight to Swim Faster	38.9	20.1	41.0
I Need to Lose Weight to Look Better	28.9	21.1	50.0

Note. SD = strongly disagree, D = disagree, N = neutral, A = agree, SA = strongly agree

Table 7.5

Drive for Thinness Among Elite Women Swimmers
(expressed in percentages)
N = 298

Variable	N	R	S	O	U	A
Eat Sweets and Carbohydrates Without Feeling Nervous	2.7	12.5	23.6	16.9	29.4	14.9
Think about Dieting	7.4	13.4	20.1	27.9	15.1	16.1
Feel Extremely Guilty after Overeating	9.4	25.5	22.5	17.4	12.4	12.8
Terrified of Gaining Weight	6.0	21.0	21.1	15.1	15.8	20.8
Exaggerate the Importance of Weight	13.8	28.5	25.5	13.8	10.4	8.1
Preoccupied with Desire to Be Thinner	12.4	23.8	25.5	11.7	10.4	16.1
Worry about Gaining Weight	18.2	33.1	22.0	10.5	8.4	7.8

Note. N = never, R = rarely, S = sometimes, O = often, U = usually, A = always

population. However, the fact that half or more reported thinking about bingeing or actually binged does seem abnormal.

Decisions of swimmers in this study about weight and weight loss seem to be based on subjective judgments rather than information. Nutrition and weight control education were not often discussed in swim programs, but swimmers were still told by their coaches to lose weight. The opinion of coaches may be especially important to these swimmers compared to opinions of family and nonathletic youths (Levinson, Powell, & Steelman, 1986). Both coaches and elite swimmers primarily used body weight and subjective "feel" to determine what best swimming weight should be. These two methods may work well for many swimmers; however, in some instances they may be unreliable. For example, female swimmers who have recently gained weight due to puberty may attempt to diet to a weight that is no longer physiologically healthy.

Pressure to lose weight, especially if negative or punitive, appears to be very detrimental to some elite women swimmers. The open-ended responses by the elite women swimmers concerning punishment for not meeting weight goals clearly indicated insensitivity and misdirected guidance on the part of some swimming coaches toward female swimmers.

Coaches sometimes use male swimmers as the standard of comparison for female swimmers. It appears that undue and errant attention is being focused on leanness of female swimmers by some coaches and swimmers. Researchers report that essential fat for men is approximately 3% (Katch, Katch, & Behnke, 1980; Stamford, 1987). Women have an additional 5%–9% essential fat which is sex specific (Katch et al., 1980; Stamford, 1987). When the sex-specific essential fat of women (5%–9%) is subtracted from the body fat of the average elite female swimmer (17.4%, Sharp, 1985), the percent body fat values of elite female swimmers (8.4%–12.4%) are comparable to that of elite male swimmers (9.1%) (Sharp, 1985). Further, the swimming literature suggests excessive leanness in swimmers is not necessarily beneficial. Counsilman (1968); Stager, Cordain, and Becker (1984); and Troup et al. (1986) point out that fat displaces less water, causing the individual to float higher in the water, thus creating less resistance and less inertia to overcome, which could be advantageous to swimmers. Research by Stager et al. (1984) reported that performance in young female swimmers was relatively independent of body fatness. Nevertheless, if a criterion is to be used, for athletes, percent body fat rather than weight is a more accurate measure of fitness for competition (Brownell & Steen, 1987; Weigley, 1984).

Rosen et al. (1986) reported that the college athletes in their study wanted to lose weight primarily to improve athletic performance (83%). In contrast, more of the elite women swimmers in this study wanted to lose weight to look better (50%) rather than to swim faster (41%). Also, contrary to the preponderance of literature on body composition (Allsen, Harrison, & Vance, 1981; Lohman, 1987; Maglischo, 1982; Ross, Pate, Lohman, & Christenson, 1987; Sinning, 1980; Weigley, 1984), the elite women swimmers in this study thought weight rather than percent body fat was more important.

Although the literature suggests that weight should be lost early in the season (Smith, 1980, 1984a, 1984b), almost half of the elite women swimmers in this study reported dieting to lose weight at the time of the Olympic Selection Meet. Concern about dieting and fear of gaining weight, coupled with frequent weighing, suggest that societal pressures, pressures from coaches, incorrect beliefs about the importance of thinness, and preoccupation with weight are widespread among these elite women athletes.

In summary, the problem of unhealthy and ineffective weight control techniques leading to bulimic-type behavior among some elite women swimmers may have its roots in swimmer or coach expectations. The swimmer may base self-concept on appearance and ability to swim fast. Since the current "fad" in both Western society and competitive sports is thinness or leanness, she may attempt to lose weight rapidly using pathogenic techniques. Coaches' reputations are built on the ability to produce fast swimmers and they may be unaware of best swimming weight, reasonable lean/fat tissue ratios for women swimmers, nutrition, and healthy weight control techniques. Unknowingly, they may encourage unhealthy behaviors from their elite women swimmers. College swimming coaches may have additional incentives to encourage leanness. They may have a monetary investment in the elite woman swimmer in the form of a scholarship, and the expectations of full scholarship swimmers are that they win. Coaches may focus on weight loss as a way to assure immediate success.

In conclusion, the results of this study appear to corroborate past studies that demonstrate concern with weight and thinness along with unhealthy eating, dieting, and weight loss patterns among athletes. As a consequence of this type of focus, some elite female swimmers may be competing at less than full strength. In addition, some lose self-esteem due to derogatory comments or punitive measures for failing to meet what may be an unfair or unhealthy *assigned* weight standard. Perhaps the most troubling finding of this study is the pervasive attitude among elite female swimmers to look well and to lose weight regardless of the method or consequence. This type of focus is not conducive to the total mental, emotional, and physical wholeness required in high level competition. Elite female swimmers cannot afford to compete internationally at less than full strength, nor should they jeopardize their future health after competitive swimming is over.

References

Allsen, P. E., Harrison, J. M., & Vance, B. (1981). *Fitness for life* (2nd ed.). Dubuque, IA: Brown.

Black, D. R., & Burckes-Miller, M. E. (1988). Male and female college athletes: Use of anorexia nervosa and bulimia nervosa weight loss methods. *Research Quarterly for Exercise and Sport, 59,* 252–256.

Borgen, J. S., & Corbin, L. B. (1987). Eating disorders among female athletes. *The Physician and Sportsmedicine, 15*(2), 89–95.

Brownell, K., & Steen, S. N. (1987). Modern methods for weight control: The physiology and psychology. *The Physician and Sportsmedicine, 15*(12), 122–137.

Burckes-Miller, M. E., & Black, D. R. (1988). Male and female college athletes: Prevalence of anorexia nervosa and bulimia nervosa. *Athletic Training, 23,* 137–140.

Clark, N., Nelson, M., & Evans, W. (1988). Nutrition education for elite female runners. *The Physician and Sportsmedicine, 18*(2), 124–134.

Combs, M. R. (1982). By food possessed. *Women's Sports, 4*(2), 12–18.

Counsilman, J. E. (1968). *The science of swimming.* Englewood Cliffs, NJ: Prentice-Hall.

Dummer, G. M., Rosen, L. W., Heusner, W. W., Roberts, P. J., & Counsilman, J. E. (1987). Pathogenic weight-control behaviors of young competitive swimmers. *The Physician and Sportsmedicine, 15*(5), 75–84.

Fleck, S. J. (1983). Body composition of elite American athletes. *Journal of Sports Medicine, 11*(6), 398–403.

Garner, D. M., Olmsted, M. P., & Polivy, J. (1984). *Manual for eating disorder inventory. (EDI).* Odessa, FL: Psychological Assessment Resources, Inc.

Green, L. W., Kreuter, M. W., Deeds, S. G., & Partridge, K. B. (1980). *Health education planning: A diagnostic approach.* Mountainview, CA: Mayfield.

Katch, F. I., Katch, V. L., & Behnke, A. R. (1980). The underweight female. *The Physician and Sportsmedicine, 8*(12), 55–60.

Levinson, R., Powell, B., & Steelman, L. C. (1986). Social location, significant others and body image among adolescents. *Social Psychology Quarterly, 49,* 330–337.

Lohman, T. G. (1987). The use of skinfold to estimate body fatness on children and youth. *Journal of Physical Education, Recreation & Dance, 58*(9), 74–77.

Lundholm, J. K., & Littrell, J. M. (1986). Desire for thinness among high school cheerleaders: Relationship to disordered eating and weight control behaviors. *Adolescence, 21*(83), 573–579.

Maglischo, E. W. (1982). *Swimming faster*. California State University, Chico: Mayfield.

Raciti, M. C., & Norcross, J. C. (1987). The EAT and EDI: Screening, interrelationships and psychometrics. *International Journal of Eating Disorders, 6*, 579–586.

Rosen, L. W., & Hough, D. O. (1988). Pathogenic weight-control behaviors of female college gymnasts. *The Physician and Sportsmedicine, 16*(9), 140–144.

Rosen, L. W., McKeag, D. B., Hough, D. O., & Curley, V. (1986). Pathogenic weight-control in female athletes. *The Physician and Sportsmedicine, 14*, 79–86.

Ross, J. G., Pate, R. R., Lohman, T. G., & Christenson, G. M. (1987). Changes in the body composition of children. *Journal of Physical Education, Recreation & Dance, 58*(9), 74–77.

Sharp, R. (1985). Nutrition. *Coaches College Resource Guide, 2*, 4–7.

Sinning, W. E. (1980). Use and misuse of anthropometric estimates of body composition. *Journal of Physical Education and Recreation, 51*, 43–45.

Smith, N. J. (1980). Excessive weight loss and food aversion in athletes simulating anorexia nervosa. *Pediatrics, 66*, 139–142.

Smith, N. J. (1984a). Weight control in the athlete. *Clinical Sports Medicine, 3*, 693–704.

Smith, N. J. (1984b). Nutrition and athletic performance. *Primary Care, 11*, 33–42.

Stager, J. M., Cordain, L., & Becker, J. (1984). Relationship of body composition to swimming performance in female swimmers. *Journal of Swimming, 1*, 21–26.

Stamford, B. (1987). What is the importance of body fat? *The Physician and Sportsmedicine, 15*(3), 216.

Troup, J., Daniels, J., McMaster, W., Campbell, L., Troup, S., Arredondo, S., Duda, L., & Richardson, A. B. (1986). *Performance profiles of developing and elite swimmers in the United States*. Colorado Springs, CO: United States Swimming, Inc.

Weigley, E. S. (1984). Average? Ideal? Desirable? A brief overview of height-weight tables in the United States. *Journal of the American Dietetic Association, 84*, 417–423.

Windsor, R. A., Baranowski, T., Clark, N., & Cutter, G. (1984). *Evaluation of health promotion and education programs*. Palo Alto, CA: Mayfield.

8

Disordered Eating Behaviors Among Synchronized Swimmers

CHRISTINE S. SMITHIES

This study investigated the prevalence and correlates of disordered eating behaviors among synchronized swimmers. Measures of eating and weight management habits, body satisfaction, and self-esteem were administered to 149 subjects who were then classified into one of seven eating groups and one of four weight groups. Few subjects were anorexic, bulimic, or purgers; however, the results indicated a high prevalence of bingers and dieters. The largest eating category was subthreshold bulimic (37.4%), followed by normal eater (28.2%), binger (20.6%), and chronic dieter (11.5%). As a whole, the sample was normal weight or underweight, yet 52% reported feeling fat on a daily basis. Normal eaters had significantly higher body satisfaction than all other groups (p< .05) and significantly higher self-esteem than subthreshold bulimics (p < .05). The implications of these findings are discussed, with special concern for the normative practice of bingeing and dieting behaviors and the high prevalence of subthreshold bulimia.

Stories abound of accomplished athletes whose efforts to regulate weight have taken the form of anorexia or bulimia. Have these stories represented the extreme experiences of a few athletes, or have they been telltale glimpses into the lives of many athletes? The purpose of this paper is to examine the prevalence of disordered eating among synchronized swimmers, participants in a sport which emphasizes a thin body appearance. This investigation was guided by a particular interest in "subthreshold" bulimics, athletes whose restricting, bingeing, and purging behaviors would not have sufficient frequency or severity to qualify them for a clinical diagnosis of bulimia according to the *Diagnostic and Statistical Manual of Mental Disorders Revised* (*DSM III-R*) (American Psychiatric Association, 1987), but who nonetheless have associated physical and/or psychological problems.

Participants in sports requiring thinness for success, such as gymnastics, may be high risk populations for the development of eating disorders (e.g., Borgen & Corbin, 1987; Boskind-White & White, 1983; Squire, 1983). Athletes in general have been identified as at risk for developing subclinical forms of eating pathology (Burckes-Miller & Black, 1988a, 1988b; Rosen & Hough, 1988; Yates, Leehey, & Shisslak, 1983), and it has been debated whether these subclinical eating disorders were truly indicative of underlying psychopathology (Mallick, Whipple, & Huerta, 1984).

Synchronized swimming, recognized as an official Olympic sport in 1984, has always been a subjectively judged sport, and like gymnastics, an athlete's appearance has been an influential factor in her evaluation (C. Davis, personal communication, October 15, 1986). At the 1986 United States Aquatics Conference, athletes representing the sport of synchronized swimming disclosed that some participants were using food restriction and purging techniques for weight control (S. Weinberg, M.D., personal communication, September 18, 1986).

There has been one prior study of eating disorders for a sample of 17 synchronized swimmers. Guthrie (1985) reported that 23.5% satisfied the criteria for bulimia of the *Diagnostic and Statistical Manual of Mental Disorders* (*DSM III*) (American Psychiatric Association, 1980) while 17% reported restricted eating associated with anorexia nervosa. The athletes who reported an eating disorder also reported that participation in their sport made their eating problem somewhat more of a problem. However, the small sample size seriously limited generalizability of the results.

In a study of 182 collegiate athletes from a variety of sports but not including synchronized swimming, Rosen, McKeag, Hough, and Curley (1986) reported that 32% of the sample practiced at least one pathogenic weight control method, including self-induced vomiting, laxatives, diet pills, or diuretics. The highest prevalence (74%) existed among gymnasts. In a survey of 41 female gymnasts, Costar (1983) reported that 61% engaged in regular binge eating and 24% used self-induced vomiting, laxatives, and/or diuretics to control or lose weight.

In this investigation, it was predicted that most of the athletes would not qualify as truly anorexic or bulimic, but that many would have bingeing and eating patterns that would distinguish them from normal eaters. A major problem encountered in eating disorder research has been how to classify individuals with subthreshold eating disorders. Fairburn and Garner (1986) described "subthreshold eating disorders" as individuals who had some or all of the *DSM III-R* symptoms of bulimia nervosa or anorexia nervosa, but who did not possess the symptoms with sufficient severity to qualify for a diagnosis of bulimic or anorexic. It has been suspected that chronic dieting, or the use of other weight control methods, may sometimes have preceded the development of a diagnosed disorder (e.g., Katzman & Wolchik, 1984; Ousley, 1986; Striegel-Moore, Silberstein, & Rodin, 1986). Furthermore, psychological distress may increase as one moves along the continuum from no weight concerns to binge eating to bulimia (Katzman & Wolchik, 1984; Mintz & Betz, 1988; Ousley, 1986).

Method

Subjects

A total of 251 questionnaires was mailed to 18 swimming clubs whose coaches were known to the investigator through informal contacts. Questionnaires were returned by 149 respondents (response rate 55.3%). The subjects represented 15 synchronized swimming teams geographically distributed throughout the United States. All subjects were women, and the sample was predominantly Anglo (93.2%). Subjects ranged in age from 10 to 22 years, and the mean age was 15.6 years. The median height was five feet, four inches, and the median weight was 120 pounds. Nineteen percent of the sample had participated in Senior Nationals, the most elite national competition, and 14.2% had been members of the United States National Synchronized Swimming Team.

Measures

Participants completed the following measures: (1)Rosenberg's (1965) Self-Esteem Scale; (2) Bohrnstedt's (1977) Body Parts Satisfaction Scale; and (3) Weight Management in Athletes Questionnaire, a survey developed for this study and adapted in part from the Michigan State University Weight Control Survey (Dummer, Rosen, Heusner, Roberts, & Counsilman, 1986) and in part from the Weight Management, Eating, and Exercise Habits Questionnaire (Ousley, 1986).

The Rosenberg Self-Esteem Scale measures the self-acceptance aspect of self-esteem and consists of ten items rated on a four-point scale ranging from one (strongly agree) to four (strongly disagree). Scores can range from zero (very low self-esteem) to four (very high self-esteem). Test-retest reliability over a 2-week period has been found to be high ($r = .85$), and the measure has been found to moderately correlate ($r = .59$) with scores on the Coopersmith Self-Esteem Inventory and with the California Psychological Inventory Self-Acceptance scale ($r = .66$) (Robinson & Shaver, 1973).

Bohrnstedt's Body Parts Satisfaction Scale (BPSS) consists of 24 body parts rated from one (extremely dissatisfied) to six (extremely satisfied). An overall body satisfaction score was determined by averaging all items, so that a score of one was indicative of extreme body dissatisfaction and a score of six was indicative of extreme body satisfaction. The internal consistency of this scale has been found to be high ($r = .89$, Noles, Cash, & Winstead, 1985). Convergent validity has been demonstrated by the correlation between the mean body satisfaction score and a single item measuring overall body satisfaction ($r = .70$, Bohrnstedt, 1977). The overall body satisfaction score has been found to moderately correlate ($r = .45$ for women, Bohrnstedt, 1977) with the Janis-Field Feelings of Inadequacy Scale (Eagly, 1967, cited in Robinson & Shaver, 1973).

The Weight Management in Athletes Questionnaire (WMAQ) designed for this study consisted of 102 items. Questions regarding subjects' health, weight-related attitudes, and sport-related attitudes were similar to items from the Michigan State University Weight Control Survey (Dummer et al., 1986). Questions regarding subjects' eating, dieting, and exercise habits were similar to items from Ousley's (1986) Weight Management, Eating, and Exercise Habits Questionnaire (WMQ). Subjects reported frequencies for using various weight control behaviors. These responses were used to classify subjects into eating categories based on an operationalized version of *DSM III* criteria for bulimia (Ousley, 1986) and revised by Mintz and Betz (1988) to reflect *DSM III-R* criteria for Bulimia Nervosa and Eating Disorder Not Specified. *DSM III-R* criteria for Anorexia Nervosa were operationalized by this investigator.

The eating categories and membership criteria included: (1) normal eater (reported no bingeing, no purging, dieting less than once per month, no excessive exercising, defined as less than 31.8 hours per week, which was one standard deviation above the sample mean for time spent per week in training plus additional exercise), (2) bulimia nervosa (8 or more binges per month, purging at least once per month or dieting at least once weekly or exercising excessively), (3) binger (any binge eating, no purging, no excessive exercising, dieting once per month or less), (4) purger (no binge eating, purging at least once per month), (5) chronic dieter (no binge eating, no purging, at least weekly dieting or over-exercising), (6) anorexic (intense fear of gaining weight, weight 15% or more below normal weight, three consecutive missed periods if menses had commenced), and (7) subthreshold bulimic (included all subjects who failed to meet criteria for any other group, for example, bingeing less than 8 times per month and weekly dieting).

Subjects were classified into one of five weight groups based on standardization of self-reports of their weights. The reported weight and height of each subject was converted to a percentage of a standard body weight score by multiplying reported weight by 100, and then dividing it by normal weight. The Metropolitan Life Insurance Tables (1987) were used to define normal weight as the mid-range for a medium-build frame, corrected for height and age, a method standardly used by other researchers in the field (e.g., Johnson, Stuckey, Lewis, & Schwartz, 1982; Mintz, 1987; Ousley, 1986). If percent of normal weight was less than or equal to 85% (this reflected *DSM III-R* weight criterion for Anorexia Nervosa), the subject was classified as under-underweight. If percent of normal weight was greater than 85% but less than or equal to 89%, the subject was classified as underweight. The normal weight classification included subjects whose percent weight fell between 90% and less than or equal to 110%. The overweight classification included subjects with percent weights greater than 100% and less than or equal to 119%. Finally, subjects were classified as obese when percent weight was greater than 119%.

Subjects were divided into four skill levels based on their highest figure score (compulsory movements in the water) at a national competition. Skill level 1 was defined as the lowest skill level, and skill level 4 was defined as the highest skill level.

Procedure

Coaches received instructions, consent forms, surveys, and debriefing materials. Participation by athletes was voluntary and anonymous. Questionnaire administration took approximately one hour. Written debriefing information regarding the problems associated with eating disorders and resource information for obtaining help was provided to the athletes. Postcards and phone calls to coaches were used as follow-up reminders.

Results

Complete data for classification of subjects into eating categories were available for 131 subjects. No subjects were classified as bulimic or purger, and only three were classified as anorexic (2.3%), supporting the prediction that few or none of the athletes would have bona fide eating disorders. However, the largest eating category consisted of 49 subjects (37.4%) who were classified as subthreshold bulimic. The second largest eating category consisted of 37 subjects (28.3%) classified as normal eaters. The third largest category consisted of 27 bingers (20.6%), and 15 athletes (11.5%) were chronic dieters. No subjects were classified in the categories for bulimia nervosa or purger. The categories of anorexia, bulimia, and purger were dropped from all subsequent analyses; thus this became an investigation of subthreshold bulimics, normal eaters, bingers, and chronic dieters.

There were 90 subjects with an official skill rating. Skill levels 1 and 2 each included 23 subjects, and skill levels 3 and 4 each included 22 subjects. These subjects were then classified in eating categories by skill levels. There were no significant differences in the distribution of eating behaviors among the skill levels, but the largest percentage of subthreshold bulimics (13.3%) were members of skill level 4, the most skilled group, and the largest percentage of normal eaters (7.8%) were members of skill level one, the least skilled group.

The frequency distributions for bingeing, dieting, and other weight control methods were calculated for the entire sample. Bingeing behavior was reported by 58% of the sample. For subjects who reported bingeing, the frequency of the behavior varied from 6% who binged at least twice per week, to 30% who binged 1–4 times per month, to 21% who binged less than once per month. Skipping meals was the most popular weight control method, reported by 58% of the subjects. Nearly half of the meal-skippers reported skipping meals at least twice per week. Calorie counting was practiced by 45% of the subjects. About half of the calorie counters reported counting calories at least twice per week. Using special diets and fasting were each reported by 25% of the subjects. The more drastic methods, including diet pills, vomiting, laxatives, and diuretics, were each reported by less than 9% of the sample.

The average time per week spent training for synchronized swimming was 12.8 hours ($SD = 8$). When time spent training for synchronized swimming was combined with time spent in other exercise, the total exercise time per week was 20.2 hours ($SD = 11.6$).

Bingeing and dieting were used with enough frequency by the entire sample to be considered normative behaviors, while the more drastic weight control methods, such as laxatives and diet pills, were used infrequently. As a whole, this sample was normal weight and underweight, yet more than half the subjects described "feeling fat" on a daily basis. Subthreshold bulimics were the heaviest subjects, although the majority of them were normal weights.

The number and percentage of subjects for each weight group by eating category are presented in Table 8.1. It should be noted that only 13 subjects (9.9%) were both normal weight and normal eaters, although 52.8% of the total sample was within the normal weight range. Twenty subjects (15.3%) were normal eaters, but were under-underweight, and 28 subjects (21.4%) were normal weight but subthreshold bulimics. Dieters also tended to be normal weight.

Univariate analyses of variance of all dependent variables as a function of membership in the four eating categories (normal, binger, chronic dieter, subthreshold bulimic) were completed. Eating category had significant effects on all body satisfaction variables, including overall body satisfaction, $F(3, 123) = 9.89$, $p < .001$; the lower torso, $F(3, 123) = 6.62$, $p < .001$; the mid-torso, $F(3, 123) = 8.26$, $p < .001$; the extremities, $F(3, 123) = 5.82$, $p < .001$; and the face factor, $F(3, 123) = 5.32$, $p < .01$. Eating category also had significant unique effects on Self-Esteem, $F(3, 124) = 3.85$, $p < .05$, Feel Fat Daily, $F(3, 124) = 6.80$, $p < .001$, Weight Affects Coach's Opinion, $F(3, 123) = 6.80$, $p < .001$, and Sport Pressures To Be Thin, $F(3, 123) = 4.86$, $p < .001$.

Table 8.2 presents means and group differences as a function of eating category. Normal eaters were significantly more satisfied with their bodies than dieters, bingers, or subthreshold bulimics; Scheffé (3, 116), 17.4, 15.2, 19.6, 17.9, $p < .05$, respectively. Normal eaters also had significantly lower percent weights than bingers, dieters, and subthreshold bulimics; Scheffé (3, 119), 16.6, 14.7, 10.4, 14.8, $p < .05$, respectively. In other words, the normal eaters were most satisfied with their bodies and were also considerably thinner than their dieting, bingeing, and subthreshold bulimic counterparts.

Table 8.1
Subjects Classified by Eating Category and Weight Group

Eating Category	Weight Group				
	Under-Under	Under-Weight	Normal	Over-Weight	Obese
Anorexic	3/2.3	0	0	0	0
Bingers	8/6.1	1/.8	16/12.2	0	2/1.5
Dieters	2/1	1/.8	10/7.8	2/1.5	0
Normal	20/15.3	4/3	13/9.9	0	0
Sub-Bulimics	4/3	12/8.9	28/21.4	2/1.5	3/2.3

Note: The first number refers to the number of subjects in each weight group by eating category, and the second number refers to the percentage of the total sample ($N = 131$).

Table 8.2

Means and Group Differences by Eating Category for Univariate Analysis of Variance Results

Variable	Normals	Dieters	Bingers	Subthreshold Bulimics
Body Satisfaction				
Total Score	4.01/.70$_a$	3.39/.54$_b$	3.53/.70$_b$	3.28/.51$_b$
Face	4.76/.73$_a$	4.21/.60$_{ab}$	4.27/.90$_{ab}$	4.07/.85$_b$
Lower Torso	4.34/1.25$_{cd}$	3.27/1.32$_c$	3.50/1.25$_{abcd}$	3.19/1.20$_{bd}$
Mid Torso	4.08/1.55$_a$	2.67/1.45$_b$	3.00/1.44$_b$	2.52/1.47$_b$
Extremities	4.80/.86$_a$	4.11/.94$_b$	4.20/1.05$_{ab}$	4.02/.80$_b$
Self-Esteem	3.35/4.15$_a$	3.10/5.40$_{ab}$	3.31/4.60$_{ab}$	3.02/4.45$_b$
Weight (in percent of Norm)	83.40/13.87$_a$	96.00/9.52$_a$	94.30/13.00$_b$	96.50/12.62$_b$
Weight Affects Opinion of Coach	1.13/.35$_a$	1.33/.62$_{ab}$	1.25/.45$_a$	1.69/.77$_b$
Sport Pressures to Be Thin	2.32/.71$_a$	1.64/.50$_b$	2.37/.69$_b$	1.67/.66$_b$
Feel Fat Daily	1.67/.47$_a$	1.53/.52$_{abc}$	1.60/.50$_a$	1.24/.43$_c$

Note: Means within each row with the same subscript were not significantly different from one another. Numbers after the slash are standard deviators.

Interpretation of Scores: Body Satisfaction scores ranged from 1 (extremely satisfied) to 6 (extremely dissatisfied); Self-Esteem Scores ranged from 1 (low self-esteem) to 4 (high self-esteem); for WMAQ Item #31, "How much does your weight affect your coach's opinion of you as an athlete?" scores ranged from 1 = My weight has very little effect, 2 = My weight has a moderate effect, 3 = My weight has a big effect; for WMAQ Item #3, "How intense is the pressure for a synchronized swimming athlete to be quite thin?" scores ranged from 1 = Pressure to be thin is intense, 2 = Pressure to be thin is moderate, 3 = There is very little or no pressure; for Item #6, "On a daily basis, do you 'feel fat'?" scores were 1 = Yes, 2 = No.

Subthreshold bulimics reported significantly lower self-esteem than normal eaters; Scheffé (3, 124), 15.0, 12.4, $p < .05$, respectively. Compared to normal eaters and bingers, significantly more subthreshold bulimics felt fat, Scheffé (3, 124), 28.3, 31.0, 35.0, $p < .05$, respectively, and had stronger beliefs that their weight affected the opinion of their coach; Scheffé (3, 123), 30.5, 35.8, 47.3, $p < .05$, respectively. Subthreshold bulimics and dieters reported significantly more sport pressure to be thin than bingers or normal eaters; Scheffé (3, 123), 45.0, 35.6, 28.6, 30.5, $p < .05$, respectively. In general, subthreshold bulimics were notably different from normal eaters, bingers, and chronic dieters.

Pearson product-moment correlation coefficients were calculated to determine the correlation between self-esteem and body satisfaction for each eating category. The relationship was strong for normal eaters, $r(36) = .68$; moderate for bingers, $r(26) = .54$, and subthreshold bulimics, $r(48) = .52$; and weak for chronic dieters, $r(14) = .14$.

Discussion

The prevalence of disordered eating behaviors among synchronized swimmers was investigated. Only three swimmers were classified as anorexic, and no one was classified as bulimic or purger, supporting the prediction that few athletes would have bona fide eating disorders. Perhaps the rigorous physical demands of synchronized swimming have precluded the participation of athletes physically weakened or psychologically impaired by extreme dieting and purging behaviors.

The largest percentage of the sample (37%) was classified as subthreshold bulimic, suggesting that these athletes may be *prebulimic*. Subthreshold bulimics had significantly lower self-esteem than normal eaters. Only 28% of the sample were normal eaters. Normal eaters weighed less, reported greater overall body satisfaction, and perceived less pressure from within the sport to be thin than all other subjects. The correlation between body satisfaction and self-esteem was also strongest for normal eaters, and in general, the correlations between self-esteem and body satisfaction were stronger for these athletes than for college women (Mintz & Betz, 1988), suggesting that normal eaters may possess greater body satisfaction and self-esteem than dieters, bingers, or subthreshold bulimics.

Most subjects practiced some constellation of dieting and bingeing behaviors (58%). The high level of bingeing may be symptomatic of chronically restricted food intake related to regular dieting (Wardle & Beinhart, 1981). This was a predominantly underweight and normal weight sample, yet 52% of the subjects reported feeling fat, and subthreshold bulimics felt fat significantly more than normal eaters or bingers.

The present findings have important implications. While bulimia and anorexia may be uncommon, chronic dieting and bingeing seem to be normative. Further research will be necessary to determine whether these behaviors are detrimental to the physical and/or psychological well-being of athletes. However, subthreshold bulimics were also the heaviest subjects, felt more pressure to be thin from within the sport than normal eaters, and had significantly lower self-esteem than normal eaters. These subthreshold bulimics seem to be at risk for developing bulimia and deserve careful attention from the coaching staff. The largest percentage of subthreshold bulimics were members of the most skilled group, and further investigation may show that advanced synchronized swimmers experience greater prevalence and/or severity of disordered eating.

Normal eaters weighed less than other subjects. Possibly they were genetically predisposed to thinness; however, it is also possible that these normal eaters were thinner *because* they were normal eaters and did not experience weight gain often associated with dieting.

Several limitations of this study ought to be noted. The sample was not chosen randomly and therefore the results should not be generalized beyond this sample. Internal validity is questionable because all data were self-reported. The response rate would possibly have been higher if questionnaires had been administered by the investigator. It also is not posssible to determine why some subjects chose not to participate in the study. Perhaps they were simply unmotivated, or perhaps they were concealing disordered eating.

In sum, it is evident that the sport of synchronized swimming is characterized by thin athletes who try to be yet thinner. These swimmers are young and impressionable women, still developing their bodies and nutritional habits. These athletes seem in need of information about dieting and nutrition. Frank consideration also must be given to the possibility that a very thin body is increasingly necessary for the execution of some of the most difficult movements in synchronized swimming (M. J. Ruggieri, personal communication, October 22, 1988). Therefore, the pressures to be exceptionally thin may increase, and more athletes may try to defy normal weights with dieting and perhaps the use of more drastic weight control methods.

References

American Psychiatric Association. (1980). *Diagnostic and statistical manual of mental disorders* (3rd ed). Washington, DC: Author.

American Psychiatric Association. (1987). *Diagnostic and statistical manual of mental disorders (3rd ed., revised).* Washington, DC: Author.

Bohrnstedt, G. W. (1977). *On measuring body satisfaction.* Unpublished manuscript, Indiana University.

Borgen, J. S., & Corbin, C. B. (1987). Eating disorders among female athletes. *The Physician and Sportsmedicine, 15*(1), 89–95.

Boskind-White, M., & White, M. (1983). *Bulimarexia.* New York: W. W. Norton and Company.

Burckes-Miller, M. E., & Black, D. R. (1988a). Behaviors and attitudes associated with eating disorders: Perceptions of college athletes about food and weight. *Health Education Research, Theory and Practice, 3,* 203–208.

Burckes-Miller, M. E., & Black, D. R. (1988b). Male and female college athletes: Prevalance of anorexia nervosa and bulimia nervosa. *Athletic Training, 23,* 137–140.

Costar, E. D. (1983). Eating disorders: Gymnasts at risk. *International Gymnast, 25,* 58–59.

Dummer, G. M., Rosen, L. W., Heusner, W. W., Roberts, P. J., & Counsilman, J. E. (1986, September 12). *Weight modification behaviors of age-group competitive swimmers.* Paper presented at the 18th Annual American Swimming Coaches Association World Clinic, Dallas, TX.

Fairburn, C. G., & Garner, D. M. (1986). The diagnosis of bulimia-nervosa. *International Journal of Eating Disorders, 5,* 403–419.

Guthrie, S. R. (1985). The prevalence and development of eating disorders within a selected intercollegiate athlete population. (Doctoral dissertation, Ohio State University, 1985). *Dissertation Abstracts International, 46,* 3649.

Johnson, C., Stuckey, M., Lewis, C., & Schwartz, D. (1982). Bulimia: A descriptive survey of 316 cases. *International Journal of Eating Disorders, 2,* 1–15.

Katzman, M. A., & Wolchik, S. A. (1984). Bulimia and binge eating in college women: A comparison of personality and behavioral characteristics. *Journal of Consulting and Clinical Psychology, 52,* 423–428.

Mallick, M. J., Whipple, T. W., & Huerta, E. (1984). *Behavioral and psychological traits of weight conscious teenagers: A comparison of eating disordered patients and high and low risk groups.* Unpublished manuscript.

Metropolitan Life Insurance Company Statistical Bulletin (1987). *58*(10), 5.

Mintz, L. B. (1987). *Prevalence and correlates of eating disordered behavior among college women.* Unpublished doctoral dissertation, The Ohio State University, Columbus, OH.

Mintz, L. B., & Betz, N. E. (1988). Prevalence and correlates of eating disordered behaviors among undergraduate women. *Journal of Counseling Psychology, 35,* 463–471.

Noles, S. W., Cash, T. F., & Winstead, B. A. (1985). Body image, physical attractiveness, and depression. *Journal of Consulting and Clinical Psychology, 53,* 88–94.

Ousley, L. (1986). *Differences among bulimic subgroups, binge eaters, and normal eaters in a female college population.* Unpublished doctoral dissertation, University of California, Santa Barbara.

Robinson, J. P., & Shaver, P. R. (1973). *Measures of social psychological attitudes* (2nd ed.). Ann Arbor, MI: Institute for Social Research.

Rosen, L. W., & Hough, D. O. (1988). Pathogenic weight control behaviors of female college gymnasts. *The Physician and Sportsmedicine, 16*(1), 141–144.

Rosen, L. W., McKeag, D. B., Hough, D. O., & Curley, V. (1986). Pathogenic weight-control behaviors in female athletes. *The Physician and Sportsmedicine, 14,* 79–86.

Rosenberg, M. (1965). *Society and the adolescent self-image.* Princeton, NJ: Princeton University Press.

Squire, S. (1983). *The slender balance.* New York: Pinnacle Books.

Striegel-Moore, R. H., Silberstein, L. R., & Rodin, J. (1986). Toward an understanding of risk factors in bulimia. *American Psychologist, 41,* 246–263.

Wardle, J., & Beinhart, H. (1981). Binge eating: A theoretical review. *British Journal of Clinical Psychology, 20,* 97–109.

Yates, A., Leehey, K., & Shisslak, C. M. (1983). Running: An analogue of anorexia? *New England Journal of Medicine, 308,* 251–255.

Author Notes

This paper is based on the author's doctoral dissertation. The author would like to acknowledge Mary Jo Ruggieri and Susan Sears, who generously gave time to this research.

9

An Exploratory Study of Eating Disorder Characteristics Among Adult Female Noncollegiate Athletes

KAREN T. SULLIVAN

DONALD H. STEEL

This study investigated psychological and behavioral characteristics of eating disorders, as well as motivation for sport participation and weight control, among a heterogeneous group of 403 female noncollegiate athletes, ages 18 to 45. Competitive athletes from rugby, running, soccer, softball, swimming, tennis, and volleyball groups, and a group of noncompetitive athletes, completed the Eating Disorder Inventory (EDI) and the Sports and Weight Control Questionnaire (SWQ) specifically designed for this investigation. The results derived from the EDI revealed that these adult female athletes were no more symptomatic of eating disorders than the women of the normative college sample. The extent of weight preoccupation, as measured by the EDI Drive for Thinness subscale, was low among the athletes (5.2%) and losing weight was not ranked by the group as a primary motive for becoming involved in sports. Physical fitness and mental well-being were primary motives for sports involvement. Athletes regarded improvements in health and appearance as the most important benefits of losing or maintaining a low body weight. Binge eating was more common among individual sport athletes than among team or racquet sport athletes. Possible tendencies toward eating disorders were indicated in 2.2% of the sample.

Substantial research attention has been devoted to studies of the prevalence of eating disorders, particularly in general college populations, but only a few studies have examined the prevalence of eating disorders specifically among athletes (Borgen & Corbin, 1987; Burckes-Miller & Black, 1988; Dummer, Rosen, Heusner, Roberts, & Counsilman, 1987; Rosen, McKeag, Hough, & Curley, 1986). Most of these studies examine collegiate competitors and the prevalence of eating disorders among these athletes is controversial. Some studies suggest a high prevalence rate while others do not. For example, Burckes-Miller and Black (1988) found in a study of 695 college athletes that 4.2% of the female athletes and 1.6% of the male athletes met the criteria for anorexia nervosa. A much greater proportion of athletes satisfied the criteria for bulimia nervosa: 39.2% of the female athletes and 14.3% of the male athletes. Certain characteristics common among those diagnosed with eating disorders, such as the use of at least one pathogenic weight loss method, were found to be higher among collegiate athletes than reported for general college and noncollege populations (Black & Burckes-Miller, 1988; Burckes-Miller & Black, 1988; Rosen & Hough, 1988; Rosen et al., 1986). Rosen et al. determined from a follow-up study of collegiate athletes that most of them engaged in pathogenic eating behaviors to improve performance and the majority believed that such techniques were harmless.

In contrast, some studies have found tendencies toward eating disorders to be no more common in athletes than nonathletes (Borgen & Corbin, 1987; Lindeboe & Slettebo, 1984). Borgen and Corbin (1987) reported no significant differences between college women athletes ($N = 67$) and nonathletes ($N = 101$) in the number of EDI subscale scores above the means of anorexics. Both groups also showed similar levels of weight preoccupation, as measured by the Eating Disorder Inventory (EDI) (Garner & Olmsted, 1984) Drive for Thinness subscale.

Differences in prevalence may be related to sport. Borgen and Corbin (1987) suggest that athletes in sports which emphasize leanness may be at high risk for developing eating disorders. Distance running is a sport where the prevalence of eating disorder symptoms may be especially elevated among collegiate (Rosen et al., 1986) and noncollegiate athletes (Clark, Nelson, & Evans, 1988; Katz, 1986; Yates, Leehey, & Shisslak, 1983). Chalmers, Catalan, Day, and Fairburn (1985) suggest that some individuals who have obsessive concerns about body weight and shape may employ exercise to a much greater extent than dieting, thus presenting another injurious variant of anorexia nervosa.

The purpose of this study was to explore the psychological and behavioral characteristics of eating disorders among adult female noncollegiate athletes who regularly practice and compete in organized community sport programs or with private clubs. Another purpose was to examine motivation for sport participation and weight control efforts. The sports in which tendencies toward eating disorders were most prevalent were also delineated.

Method

Subjects

Subjects were volunteers recruited at organized athletic team practices and competitions in the Washington, DC metropolitan area. Volunteers were assured of anonymity and were asked to complete the surveys alone and as carefully, completely, and honestly as possible. The response rate was approximately 70%. Nearly 80% of the volunteers completed the surveys on site and then placed them in a collection envelope rather than handing them directly to the researcher. The remainder were returned by mail in self-addressed, stamped envelopes provided by the investigator.

Most runners, swimmers, rugby, and tennis players were members of private sport clubs or teams. These subjects were approached at competitive events. Three different local road races (a Congressional Staff Club 10 Kilometer Run, a Footlockers Partners 8 Kilometer Race, and a 24 hour relay), a long course (50 meter) swimming meet (the DC Masters East Coast Long Course Swimming Championships), a rugby tournament, and a tennis tournament (the United Cerebral Palsy Tennis Classic) were the competitions from which athletes were recruited. All swimmers at the swim competition were members of United States Masters Swimming. All tennis players at the tournament were members of the United States Tennis Association and were from the Mid-Atlantic region. The team sport athletes from soccer, volleyball, and softball were recruited at the practices or competitions of community leagues. Team coaches or captains gave permission to address the team and ask members to fill out the surveys on site. Noncompetitive sports participants were obtained, in large part, by distribution of surveys at the U.S. Department of Justice Fitness Center.

A total of 418 subjects completed the two questionnaires employed in this study. None of the athletes were currently competing at the college level. Fifteen subjects were ages 46 to 69 years. Because eating disorders are believed to be largely a problem of the young and the sample over 45 was small, the study was limited to 403 subjects, ages 18 to 45. The average age for these subjects was 29.3 years.

Twenty-five of the survey respondents reported on one of the questionnaires that they regularly participated in sports but did not compete. They were analyzed as the noncompetitive sample. Three hundred and seventy competitors represented the following seven sports: rugby ($n = 25$), soccer ($n = 75$), swimming ($n = 53$), running ($n = 63$), tennis ($n = 29$), softball ($n = 30$), and volleyball ($n = 95$). The number for each group reflects those who reported the respective sport as their primary sport. Eight competitors listed cycling ($n = 4$), racquetball ($n = 3$), or rowing ($n = 1$) as their primary sport, even though they were recruited at practices or competitions of the other seven sports. Meaningful analyses of these three sport groups could not be conducted due to small sample sizes. Thus, the analysis of competitive athletes was limited to 370 athletes from seven primary sport groups. These competitors were subdivided into three age groups: 18 to 25 years ($n = 120$), 26 to 35 years ($n = 181$), and 36 to 45 years ($n = 69$).

All subjects, both competitors and noncompetitors, exercised at least three days per week for at least 30 minutes each session. No upper limit of training was established and some subjects exercised an average of two to three hours per day. The time spent per week participating in one's primary sport ranged from an average of 4 hours and 38 minutes for rugby players to an average of 6 hours and 39 minutes for tennis players. The majority of the athletes were single ($n = 252$, 62.5%) rather than married ($n = 125$, 31.0%) or divorced/separated ($n = 15$, 3.7%). There were 11 subjects (2.7%) who did not report marital status. Over half of the survey respondents reported professional occupations ($n = 226$, 56.1%); 90 (22.3%) reported blue collar or clerical jobs, 47 (11.7%) were students, housewives, or unemployed, and 37 (9.2%) indicated occupations that were difficult to categorize (e.g., self-employed). Only 3 (0.7%) failed to note their occupation.

Procedure

Questionnaires. The Eating Disorder Inventory (EDI) and a Sports and Weight Control Questionnaire (SWQ) were administered. The EDI is a standardized psychological self-report instrument consisting of 64 questions which examine psychological and behavioral correlates of eating disorders (Garner & Olmsted, 1984). Higher scores on each of the eight subscales of the EDI (Drive for Thinness, Bulimia, Body Dissatisfaction, Ineffectiveness, Perfectionism, Interpersonal Distrust, Interoceptive Awareness, and Maturity Fears) indicate closer resemblance to individuals with clinically diagnosed eating disorders.

The Sports and Weight Control Questionnaire (SWQ), designed specifically for this study, was divided into two parts (see Appendix 9.A). The first section presented questions regarding the subjects' involvement in sport and the reasons why they had become involved in their primary sport. The second section examined eating and dieting behaviors, including binge eating (defined on the survey as "excessive, uncontrolled eating'') and purging, and posed questions directed at determining whether sport involvement was initiated in order to lose weight or was influenced by concerns about losing weight. A rank ordering of the potential benefits of losing or maintaining a low body weight was also requested.

Data Analyses. Analyses of the data were conducted in various ways. First, two-tailed one-sample *t*-tests were used to determine if there were significant differences between the means for the entire sample of 403 women athletes and the normative means for the EDI subscales. The sample then was subdivided into groups according to competitiveness, age, and primary sport group, and the subgroups were compared to the normative means. A Multivariate Analysis of Variance was used to determine the main effects and interaction effects of the three age categories and seven primary sport groups for each of the eight subscales of the EDI.

Frequencies, percentages, and means of the data from the SWQ were tabulated for the entire sample and the subsamples. Chi squared tests were used to compare responses of different subgroups on the SWQ. Finally, three subgroups of subjects who reported frequent bingeing and/or who had elevated EDI subscale scores were delineated and examined. *T*-tests were used to compare each of these groups to the EDI normative data for female college students or anorexics.

Results

Analysis of EDI Scores

Total Sample. Results indicated that the women athletes were no more symptomatic of anorexia or bulimia than were the women in the normative college sample from the EDI. Table 9.1 shows that the means of the sample in this study were lower than the normative means for female college students on each of the eight subscales of the EDI, $p <$ .005.[1] The sample means are visually represented in Figure 9.1 as well as normative data for female college students and anorexics.

Weight Preoccupation. In an earlier study, Garner, Olmsted, Polivy, and Garfinkel (1984) defined ''weight preoccupied'' as those subjects who scored 15 or higher on the Drive for Thinness subscale of the EDI.

---

[1]The probability level for the *t*-test comparisons with the EDI norms was set at .05 in order to reduce the possibility of making a Type 1 error.

Table 9.1

Comparison of EDI Normative Data with Results for Various Noncollegiate Athlete Subgroups

Groups	n	Drive Thinness	Bulimia	Body Dissatisfaction	Ineffectiveness	Perfectionism	Interpersonal Distrust	Interoceptive Awareness	Maturity Fears
Female College Students	271	5.1	1.7	9.7	2.3	6.4	2.4	2.3	2.2
EDI Normative Data									
Sample Data									
Total Sample	403	3.6^a/4.8	1.0^a/1.9	8.2^a/7.1	1.3^a/2.5	5.8^a/4.2	1.8^a/2.3	1.5^a/2.8	1.2^a/1.7
Competitors	370	3.5^a/4.6	1.0^a/1.9	8.2^a/7.1	1.2^a/2.4	5.8^a/4.2	1.8^a/2.3	1.5^a/2.8	1.2^a/1.7
Noncompetitors	25	3.8/5.8	1.1/1.7	6.6/6.4	2.4/3.7	5.8/4.2	1.4/1.9	1.6/2.7	1.3/2.0
18–25 years old	120	4.2/5.1	1.1^a/2.1	9.0/7.7	1.2^a/2.2	5.9/4.1	1.9/2.5	1.8/2.8	1.5^a/2.1
Soccer	75	3.5^a/5.2	0.4^a/1.0	9.3/7.3	1.3^a/1.8	5.5/3.9	2.0/2.2	1.0^a/1.7	1.3^a/1.7
Swimming	53	4.2/4.9	1.2/2.2	7.7/7.6	1.5/2.6	6.2/4.1	1.8/2.3	1.5/2.9	1.0^a/1.7
Running	63	3.5/5.0	1.1/2.3	6.4^a/6.4	1.0^a/1.8	5.3/3.9	1.9/2.1	1.6/3.1	0.8^a/1.3
Tennis	29	2.9/3.8	0.4^a/0.8	7.0^a/7.0	1.7/3.8	8.3^a/4.1	1.9/2.5	1.6/2.5	0.9^a/1.2
Softball	30	4.6/4.9	1.8/2.7	9.8/7.4	1.7/3.8	6.1/5.1	2.3/3.1	2.4/4.8	2.0/1.9
Volleyball	95	3.3^a/4.2	1.1/2.1	8.9/7.2	0.9^a/1.6	5.4/4.0	1.4^a/2.3	1.2^a/2.1	1.3^a/1.7
Rugby	25	2.5^a/3.7	0.6^a/1.0	7.2/6.7	1.4/2.7	6.1/4.6	2.1/2.7	2.6/3.6	1.2/2.0

Note: Numbers preceding the slash are mean scores and numbers after the slash are standard deviations.
[a] p < .005.

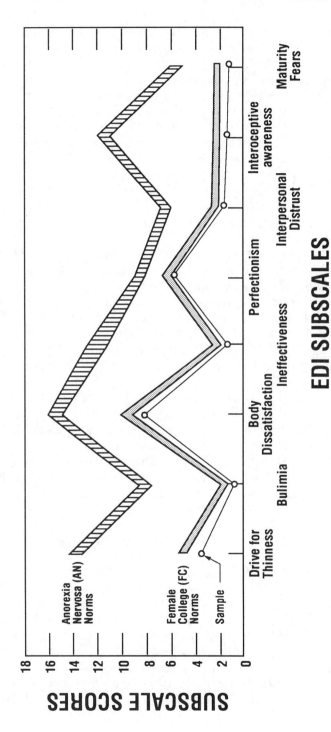

Figure 9.1. EDI subscale means for the sample of this study (*N* = 403) compared to the normative means for anorexics (*N* = 155) and female college students (*N* = 271).

This score corresponded to the 94th percentile of the normative sample of female college students. In the current sample, only 21 respondents (5.2%) met this criteria for "weight preoccupied."

Competitors and Noncompetitors. Mean EDI subscale scores for competitors ($N = 370$) and noncompetitors ($N = 25$) were calculated separately. T-tests showed that the means for the sample of 370 competitors were significantly lower than the normative means, $p < .005$, on all subscales except Perfectionism. Means for noncompetitors were similar to the normative means on all subscales. Because the noncompetitive sample was small and their mean subscale scores were similar to those of competitors, further analyses using the EDI were conducted only on the competitive sample.

Age Groups and Primary Sport Groups. An analysis of the sample of younger competitive subjects, ages 18 to 25 ($n = 120$), revealed that this group also appeared to be asymptomatic of eating disorders compared to a college sample. EDI subscale means for the seven sport groups were consistently near or significantly below the normative means.

Age by Sport. Multivariate Analyses of Variance (MANOVA) showed differences among primary sport groups. The groups differed on the Bulimia, $F(6, 363) = 2.50$, $p < .05$, Body Dissatisfaction, $F(6, 363) = 2.14$, $p < .05$, and Maturity Fears subscales, $F(6, 363) = 2.69$, $p < .05$. Student-Newman-Keuls post-hoc tests (SNK) indicated that on the Bulimia subscale, the mean for the softball group was significantly higher than the means for the rugby, soccer, and tennis groups, SNK (6, 363), 1.27, 1.39, and 1.45, $p < .05$, respectively. On the Maturity Fears subscale, the softball group scored significantly higher than swimmers, tennis players, and runners, SNK (6, 363), 1.02, 1.10, and 1.17, $p < .05$, respectively. Post hoc analyses did not reveal significant differences on Body Dissatisfaction, but softball players scored highest ($M = 9.80$) and runners scored lowest ($M = 6.43$).

Analysis of the Sports and Weight Control Questionnaire Responses

Binge Eating. Approximately one-fourth of the total sample reported binge eating and 45.8% of those, or 12.2% of the total sample, reported bingeing two to three times per month or more often. A chi-squared test indicated no significant differences between age groups in the number of bingeing incidents reported. However, there were significant differences between sport groups in the number who reported eating binges, $x^2(6, N = 370) = 20.59$, $p = .002$. As shown in Table 9.2, the rugby group contained the lowest percentage of bingers (4%) while the groups of runners and swimmers contained the highest percentages (39.7% and

Table 9.2

Number (Percentage) of Subjects in Primary Sport Groups Who Report Binge Eating and Frequency

	Rugby (n = 25)	Soccer (n = 75)	Swimming (n = 53	Running (n = 63)	Tennis (n = 29)	Softball (n = 30)	Volley-ball (n = 95)
BINGE							
Yes	1(4)	14(19)	20(38)	25(40)	6(21)	8(27)	19(20)
No	25(96)	61(81)	33(62)	38(60)	23(79)	22(73)	76(80)
FREQUENCY							
1/day+	0(0)	1(1)	0(0)	0(0)	0(0)	0(0)	0(0)
1/day	0(0)	0(0)	0(0)	0(0)	0(0)	0(0)	1(1)
4–6/week	0(0)	1(1)	0(0)	0(0)	0(0)	1(3)	0(0)
2–3/week	0(0)	0(0)	2(4)	3(5)	0(0)	1(3)	1(1)
1/week	1(4)	1(1)	3(6)	6(10)	1(3)	1(3)	1(1)
2–3/month	0(0)	2(3)	5(9)	4(6)	1(3)	1(3)	5(5)
1/month	0(0)	1(1)	1(2)	6(10)	1(3)	1(3)	5(5)
less often	0(0)	6(8)	5(9)	3(5)	2(7)	3(10)	4(4)
other	0(0)	2(3)	4(8)	3(5)	1(3)	0(0)	2(2)
none	24(96)	61(81)	33(62)	38(60)	23(79)	22(73)	76(80)

Note. Percentages were rounded to the nearest whole number.

37.7%, respectively). The youngest age group and the runners showed the highest percentages of bingeing two to three times per month or more (54.3% and 52.0%, respectively). The tendency of the youngest age group to binge more and the higher bingeing reported by runners and swimmers is especially highlighted by the finding that 9 of the 13 swimmers (69.2%) and 9 of the 20 runners (45.0%) in the youngest age group reported bingeing.

Weight Loss Methods. Table 9.3 shows the methods of weight loss used by the entire sample and various subgroups. "Increased exercise" was by far the most common method of weight control with approximately half or more of all groups reporting its use. Notably, 90% ($n = 9$) of all the primary sport competitors who reported the use of vomiting were runners. Swimmers and runners together accounted for 85.7% ($n = 6$) of those who used laxatives. As many as 14.3% ($n = 9$) of all runners vomited to lose weight and 3.2% ($n = 2$) used laxatives to lose weight. Laxatives were used to lose weight by 7.5% ($n = 4$) of all swimmers. No significant differences were found between the primary sport groups in the use of semistarvation diets, fasting, increased exercise, diet pills, or "other" weight control methods. Thirty per cent of

Table 9.3

Number and Percentage (in whole numbers) of Subjects in the Total Sample, Sport Groups, and Three Cohorts[a] Who Used Various Weight Loss Methods

				Methods of Weight Loss				
	Diets	Fasting	Exercise	Diuretic	Laxative	Vomiting	Pills	Other
Total	62(15)	24(6)	230(57)	8(2)	9(2)	11(3)	14(4)	78(19)
Competitors	56(15)	23(6)	213(58)	7(2)	7(2)	10(3)	14(4)	73(20)
Noncompetitors	5(20)	1(4)	12(48)	1(4)	1(4)	1(4)	0	6(24)
Soccer	11(15)	5(7)	48(64)	2(3)	0	0	4(5)	19(25)
Swimming	4(8)	2(4)	31(59)	1(2)	4(8)	0	3(6)	16(30)
Running	9(14)	4(6)	34(54)	1(2)	2(3)	9(14)	2(3)	10(16)
Tennis	4(14)	3(10)	16(55)	1(3)	0	0	0	7(24)
Softball	9(30)	3(10)	17(57)	1(3)	0	0	2(7)	2(7)
Volleyball	15(16)	6(6)	55(58)	1(1)	1(3)	1(1)	3(3)	15(16)
Rugby	4(16)	0	12(48)	0	0	0	0	4(16)
Cohort 1[a]	12(25)	4(8)	37(76)	1(2)	6(12)	7(14)	7(14)	13(27)
Cohort 2[a]	8(5)	2(13)	12(75)	0	3(19)	4(25)	3(19)	2(13)
Cohort 3[a]	5(56)	1(11)	8(89)	0	3(33)	4(44)	3(33)	2(22)

Note. "Diets" refers to semistarvation diets, i.e., under 1000 kcal per day; "Exercise" refers to increasing exercise specifically to reduce body fat; "Pills" refers to the use of diet pills. The most typical "other" method of weight control was restriction of certain foods or drinks, e.g., desserts, alcoholic beverages, "junk" foods, chocolate, carbohydrates, or fats, or using special diets such as the Scarsdale diet, Herbalife, fiber diet, Weight Watchers, Diet Center, Nutrisystem, the diet exchange, protein diet, or doctor prescribed diet.

[a]Cohort 1 (n = 49) includes subjects who binge two to three times per month or more; Cohort 2 (n = 16) includes subjects with elevated scores on four or more subscales of the EDI; Cohort 3 (n = 9) includes subjects who are members of both Cohorts 1 and 2.

softball players reported using semistarvation diets although no more than 16% of any other primary sport group used this method.

Approximately one-fourth of the entire sample became involved in exercise in order to lose weight. Almost twice the percentage of non-competitors (40%) compared to competitors (21%) initiated exercise in order to lose weight. This difference was significant, $X^2(1, N = 335) = 3.78, p = .05$.

Dieting Behavior and Motives for Dieting and Exercise. A question about frequency of weighing was designed as a measure of concern about body weight. The majority of the subjects (80%) reported weighing themselves three times per week or less. The majority of the subjects (85.6%) had dieted at least once since age 18, but considerably fewer were currently dieting (35.2%). The typical amount of weight loss desired in a diet was 10 pounds or less. Of the total sample, 41% indicated that their attempt to diet was influenced by their involvement in sports and 53% felt that losing weight would be a significant means to improve performance in their sport(s).

Age was not a significant factor affecting responses to the dieting behavior questions. Further, significant differences were found among the primary sport groups only on the extent of current dieting, $X^2 (6, N = 303) = 17.25, p = .008)$. The percentage of each sport group who reported current dieting ranged from 8% of rugby players to 43.3% of softball players. Two other team sport groups, volleyball and soccer, also reported high percentages of athletes who were currently dieting, 42.1% and 41.3%, respectively.

There was a trend toward significant differences among sport groups in terms of whether sport participation was initiated in order to lose weight and whether participants felt that losing weight would improve performance, $X^2 (6, N = 313) = 11.74, p = .07$, and $X^2 (6, N = 314) = 11.88, p = .06$, respectively. On both questions the highest percentage of affirmative responses was obtained for the runners (33.3% and 61.9%, respectively).

A question designed to determine the relative importance of losing weight or body fat as a motive for exercise produced results indicating that losing weight or body fat was not ranked high by the total sample or any age or sport group. Health-related motives for exercise were ranked as most important to the athletes. On the average, "physical fitness" was the foremost reason and "to feel better mentally/relax" was the second ranked reason for sport involvement provided by the entire sample. To "lose weight/fat" was ranked fifth.

Subjects with Eating Disordered Behavior and/or Attitudes

In an effort to investigate the tendency toward eating disorders, three cohorts were selected based on certain criteria expected among eating disordered patients. The first cohort included those who reported binge eating at least two to three times per month. The second cohort was based on EDI subscale scores that were associated primarily with the psychological and attitudinal characteristics of eating disorders. The third cohort met the criteria for both the first and second cohorts. Figure 9.2 shows the results of these three cohorts compared to normative means for female college students and anorexics.

The first cohort (Cohort 1; $n = 49$; 12.2% of the total sample) reported scores closely resembling female college student norms. Drive for Thinness, Bulimia, Body Dissatisfaction, and Interoceptive Awareness, however, were all above female college student normative means.

The second cohort (Cohort 2; $n = 16$; 4.0% of the total sample) had elevated scores (i.e., 1 SD above normative mean) on four to six of the EDI subscales. The third cohort (Cohort 3; $n = 9$; 2.2% of the total sample) as well as Cohort 2 reported scores most similar to anorexics rather than female college students. The subjects of Cohort 2 had mean scores similar to known anorexics (restricters and bulimics) on the Drive for Thinness, Body Dissatisfaction, Perfectionism, and Interoceptive Awareness subscales, but lower than the total anorexic group norms on the remaining four subscales. Cohort 3 revealed elevations on the same four EDI subscales as well as the Bulimia subscale.

Swimmers, runners, and softball players, as well as the younger age groups, were disproportionately represented in all three cohorts. All three cohorts reported more dieting and used every method of weight control, except diuretics, to a greater extent than the entire sample (see Table 9.3). Additionally, subjects in these three cohorts seemed to have different reasons for participating in sports from the rest of the sample. For example, more of these subjects became involved in sports in order to lose weight (31%, 50%, and 44% for Cohorts 1, 2, and 3, respectively, compared to 24% for the entire sample), felt that sports involvement influenced their dieting attempts (57%, 81%, and 67% compared to 41%), and believed that losing weight would improve their sport performance (67%, 63%, and 78% compared to 53%).

Losing weight was ranked first, second, and third as a reason for sport participation by Cohorts 3, 2, and 1, respectively. This same reason was ranked fifth by the entire sample. Cohort 3 cited improved competitive performance as the second most important reason for losing or maintaining a low body weight, whereas Cohorts 1 and 2 and the sample as a whole ranked it fourth. Thus it appeared that the members

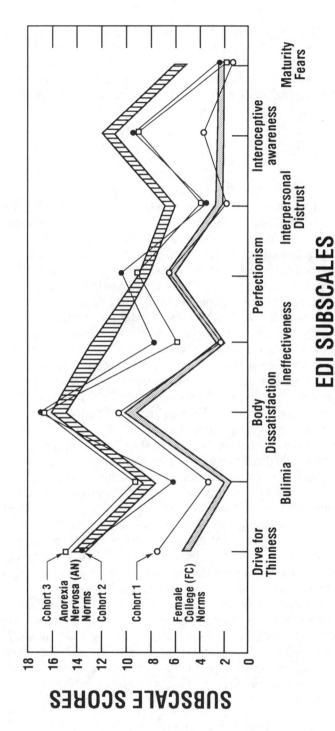

EDI SUBSCALES

Figure 9.2. EDI subscale means for the three cohorts compared to the normative means for anorexics (*N* = 155) and female college students (*N* = 271).

of Cohort 3 were participating in a primary sport mainly to lose weight and, at the same time, they believed that an important benefit of losing weight was an improvement in their competitive performance. The desire to improve appearance was the secondary motivator for their sports participation but the primary motivator for their efforts to lose or maintain a low body weight.

Discussion

The analysis of the 403 women athletes as a single sample, or subdivided into several samples by factors of age, competitiveness, and sport group membership, revealed that all of the groups of athletes in this study, as measured by the EDI, were no more symptomatic of eating disorders than the female college sample from which the normative data were derived. This suggests that, with respect to the variables measured by the EDI, the present sample of adult, noncollegiate athletes is even further removed from the pathology of eating disorders than a normal college sample. Borgen and Corbin (1987) reported similar findings, that tendencies toward eating disorders (using EDI) were not especially common in some groups of athletes. Interestingly, however, Cohorts 1, 2, and 3 approximated anorexic norms on several subscales of the EDI. This may indicate, as others have suggested (cf. Black & Burckes-Miller, 1988; Rosen et al., 1986), that there is a subset of athletes who are *at risk* for developing eating disorders.

The major contribution of the present study was the uniqueness of the sample. In this heterogeneous group of noncollegiate women athletes, whose average age was notably older than that of most groups studied, weight preoccupation was found to be low. Concern with being fashionably thin appeared to diminish with age, which may help explain a decreased risk for eating disorders. The older average age of the subjects in this study compared to the athletes in other studies may explain the low prevalence of characteristics of eating disorders in this group. However, the average age of the subjects of this study was comparable to that in another study in which elite runners showed substantial evidence of abnormal eating behaviors (Clark et al., 1988). Competitive runners, who comprised only 17.0% ($n = 63$) of the competitors in this study and 15.6% of the total sample, may be more inclined to be preoccupied with their weight. Also it is possible that elite athletes of any age engage in comparably intense training and share similar types of goals and expectations which may, in turn, influence eating and dieting behaviors.

This study did not provide evidence that the competitiveness of adult women athletes encourages the development of eating disorders. Many of the collegiate athletes in other studies (e.g., Borgen & Corbin, 1987; Rosen & Hough, 1988; Rosen et al., 1986) indicated a lack of knowledge of sound dietary practices, but also reported that they were concerned with nutrition and/or body weight because of an interest in improving athletic performance. The current sample did not generally regard improving athletic performance as a primary motive for losing or maintaining a low body weight. Perhaps for most younger athletes, competitive sport tends to be a more central and important activity in their lives and thus is one for which they are willing to make considerable sacrifices. Athletic pursuits are a top priority for only a few older competitors. Additionally, younger collegiate or high school athletes may have been coached by individuals who were intensely involved in their training, whereas older athletes may be self-coached or have coaches who are less actively involved. Hence, pressure from a coach to lose weight is less likely to be a factor for postcollegiate athletes. Also, the adult noncollegiate athlete will not be influenced by pressures to earn or retain an athletic scholarship. Finally, knowledge and education may be factors which explain differences in dietary practices between younger and older athletes. Adult noncollegiate competitors comprise a diverse group of athletes; hence, future studies of this population may be improved by considering the athletes' depth of involvement, intensity of training, extent of coaching received, and level of knowledge regarding nutrition and weight control.

Primary sport group membership was a factor in some of the differences in EDI scores and SWQ responses regarding binge eating and weight control methods. Results of the present study suggest that tendencies toward eating disorders may be more common in individual sports, such as running and swimming, as well as in softball. Bingeing among the runners and swimmers may have been related to the very high energy expenditure involved in their training. It may be, however, that individuals with a tendency toward eating disorders are drawn to these high energy consuming sports to use them as a form of purging. Zucker et al. (1985) have suggested that sports are more likely to attract people with eating disorders than to produce them. Ullyot (1986) has noted that because hyperactivity is one of the primary symptoms of anorexia nervosa, "it's no surprise that many anorexics find refuge on track and cross-country teams, where their thinness is envied—even praised—and their fast times and constant training are admired" (p. 22). The question of whether participation in certain sports encourages pathogenic weight control behaviors or whether sports attract eating disordered individuals remains to be resolved.

Data from the present investigation indicated that 12.2% of the total sample reported bingeing two to three times per month or more often. Rosen et al. (1986) used a stricter definition of bingeing but found a higher percentage (20%) of their female college athletes who reported bingeing. The age of the subjects and/or a longer period of time developing rapport with the athletes may explain the higher rate of bingeing found by Rosen and colleagues. Under-reporting may have occurred in the present study, because sufficient time was not spent with the athletes to build rapport and to assure their trust. However, the difference between the studies may not be as much a consequence of methods used as an indication that noncollegiate athletes have different (perhaps less severe) problems related to eating and dieting compared to collegiate athletes.

Improved health and appearance were cited as the primary reasons to lose or maintain a low body weight for the athletes in the present study. Health-related motives were also the foremost reasons for sport participation for the total sample. For the subjects in the present study who most closely resembled eating disordered patients, the desire to improve appearance was their most important motive for seeking to lose or maintain a low body weight, and losing weight was their primary reason for participating in sports. This subgroup of athletes believed that an additional important benefit of losing or maintaining a low body weight would be athletic performance enhancement.

Athletes in certain sport groups may be at a higher risk of having or developing eating disorders. The athlete who engages in a vigorous individual sport may use the sport predominately to control body weight and/or purge, while simultaneously being able to isolate herself in the self-absorbed pursuit of greater control of her weight. The individual who is drawn to a sport primarily to lose weight, and who regards losing weight as more crucial for appearance and sports performance than for health, is one who should be observed to determine if weight control concerns are excessive and potentially pathogenic.

In conclusion, there is ample reason to remain optimistic regarding the general psychological well-being of female athletes. The women of this study reported health concerns to be top-ranked motives for both sport participation and efforts at weight control. Genuine concern with personal health coupled with adequate knowledge of healthy dietary practices hopefully will reduce the likelihood of engaging in the hazardous behaviors characteristic of those with eating disorders. For younger athletes, where tendencies toward eating disorders appear more common, the prevention of eating disorders may be facilitated by placing greater emphasis on the value of improved health as a consequence of effective weight control and moderate sports participation.

References

Black, D. R., & Burckes-Miller, M. E. (1988). Male and female college athletes: Use of anorexia nervosa and bulimia nervosa weight loss methods. *Research Quarterly for Exercise and Sport, 59*, 252–256.

Borgen, J., & Corbin, C. (1987). Eating disorders among female athletes. *The Physician and Sportsmedicine, 15*(2), 89–95.

Burckes-Miller, M. E., & Black, D. R. (1988). Male and female college athletes: Prevalence of anorexia nervosa and bulimia nervosa. *Athletic Training, 23*(2), 137–140.

Clark, N., Nelson, M., & Evans, W. (1988). Nutrition education for elite female runners. *The Physician and Sportsmedicine, 16*(2), 124–136.

Dummer, G., Rosen, L., Heusner, W., Roberts, P., & Counsilman, J. (1987). Pathogenic weight-control behaviors of young competitive swimmers. *The Physician and Sportsmedicine, 15*(5), 75–84.

Garner, D. M., Olmsted, M. P., & Polivy, J. (1984). *Manual for eating disorder inventory (EDI)*. Odessa, FL: Psychological Assessment Resources, Inc.

Garner, D. M., Olmsted, M. P., Polivy, J., & Garfinkel, P. E. (1984). Comparison between weight-preoccupied women and anorexia nervosa. *Psychosomatic Medicine, 46*, 255–266.

Katz, J. (1986). Long distance running, anorexia nervosa, and bulimia: A report of two cases. *Comprehensive Psychiatry, 27*, 74–78.

Lindeboe, C., & Slettebo, M. (June, 1984). Are young female gymnasts malnourished? *European Journal of Applied Physiology, 52*, 457–462.

Rosen, L., & Hough, D. (1988). Pathogenic weight-control behaviors of female college gymnasts. *The Physician and Sportsmedicine, 16*(9), 140–146.

Rosen, L., McKeag, D., Hough, D., & Curley, V. (1986). Pathogenic weight-control behavior in female athletes. *The Physician and Sportsmedicine, 14*(1), 79–86.

Ullyot, J. (1986, May). How thin is too thin? *Runner's World*, 22–23.

Yates, A., Leehey, K., & Shisslak, C. (1983). Running: An analogue of anorexia? *The New England Journal of Medicine, 308*, 251–255.

Zucker, P., Avener, J., Bayder, S., Brotman, A., Moore, K., & Zimmerman, J. (1985). Eating disorders in young athletes. *The Physician and Sportsmedicine, 13*(11), 88–106.

Author Notes

Preparation of this chapter was supported in part by the American Alliance for Health, Physical Education, Recreation and Dance.

Appendix 9.A

Sports and Weight Control Questionnaire

Part I

There are numerous reasons why people become involved in sports just as there are many reasons why athletes may be concerned about body weight. This is Part I of a series of questions which examine the extent of and reasons for your sports involvement and any concerns you may have regarding weight control.

1. Are you currently involved in competitive sports?
   Yes _____   No _____ (If no, skip to question 4)

2. Circle the name(s) of the sport(s) in which you are currently competing and write the number of years you have competed on the line beside the sport.

   _____ soccer   _____ tennis   _____ body building
   _____ swimming   _____ golf   _____ triathloning
   _____ running   _____ softball   _____ cycling
   _____ track & field
   _____ others (please list)_____

3. Please fill in the names of the sports you consider to be your primary and secondary sports and indicate the extent of your athletic training in each sport.

	Primary sport	Secondary sport
	(name)	(name)
Number of workouts per week		
Average time per workout		
Intensity (please check		
hard		
medium		
easy		

   If relevant, distance covered per week, on the average (e.g., miles run or cycled, yds. or meters swum)

   If relevant, what is the primary distance at which you prefer to compete? (e.g., 10 "K" runs, marathons, open water distance swims, 100–200 meter swim sprints, etc.)

4. Please list other sport or exercise activities in which you regularly participate but do not compete and the extent of your involvement in each.

Sports	# yrs involved	# workouts/ week	ave. time/ workout	intensity (hard, medium, easy)

5. Below are some of the reasons people commonly give for participating in sports. Rank them in their order of importance to you for your primary sport.

If there is a reason not listed which is especially important to you, write it in under "other" and rank it appropriately. (Use #1 as your top ranking.)

_____ to gain muscle/look "defined"
_____ to lose weight/body fat
_____ to improve my appearance
_____ for physical fitness
_____ for competition
_____ for social reasons
_____ to feel better mentally (relax, clear mind, etc.)
_____ for fun and excitement
_____ other _____

Part II

Below are a number of questions related to weight control and weight concerns of athletes.

1. How many times per week, on the average, do you weigh yourself?
   _____ per week

2. (a) Have you attempted to lose weight or diet since turning 18?
       Yes _____ No _____(If no, skip to #6)

   (b) Are you currently dieting (within the last six months)?
       Yes _____ No _____

   (c) If you have ever or are currently dieting, approximately how many pounds have you typically wanted to lose?
       Circle: 1–5 lbs., 6–10 lbs., 11–15 lbs., 16–20 lbs., 21–25 lbs., over 26 lbs.

3. Did you get involved in sports in order to lose weight?
   Yes _____ No _____

4. Was your attempt to diet or lose weight influenced by your involvement in sport(s)?   Yes _____ No _____

5. In the sport(s) in which you participate, do you feel that losing weight would be a significant means to improve your performance?   Yes _____ No _____

6. There are a number of reasons why people may be concerned about body weight/fat. Most of the concerns are based on beliefs that certain benefits will be obtained from losing or maintaining a low body weight. Rank the following statements in order of importance to you as potential benefits of losing or maintaining a low body weight.

   _____ I will look better.
   _____ I will compete more successfully.
   _____ I will be healthier.
   _____ I will enjoy athletic participation more.
   _____ I will be at an advantage socially.
   _____ I will have higher self-esteem.
   _____ Other (please explain) _____

Continued on next page

7.   A number of recent studies have shown a large proportion of subjects reporting binge eating episodes. Most of the research has focused on college or high school populations. Little has been done to determine the extent of binge eating among populations beyond college age.

Do you ever binge (excessive, uncontrolled eating)?   Yes ____ No ____

8.   If so, approximately how often, on the average?

more than once a day____	once a week____
once a day____	2–3 times per month____
4–6 times per week ____	once a month____
2–3 times per week ____	less often ____

other (e.g., in cycles or spurts; please explain):
_____

9.   Since losing weight may be very difficult, people may try a variety of methods to assist them in reaching their weight goal. Do you currently use one or more of the following to help you control your weight (please check)? If so, for each one checked, please indicate how many times per month, on the average, you use the method checked.

Method	Frequency (times per month)
____ semistarvation diets (less than 1000 calories/day)	____
____ starving/fasting	____
____ increased exercise	____
____ diuretics	____
____ laxatives	____
____ vomiting	____
____ diet pills	____
____ none of the above	____
____ other ____	____

10

Relationship of Self-Concept, Eating Behavior, and Success of Female Collegiate Gymnasts from Big Ten Conference Teams

VALERIE A. UBBES

This investigation explored the relationship between self-concept and eating behavior among 56 female collegiate gymnasts from six Big Ten Conference teams. The Collegiate Gymnastic Profile, Tennessee Self-Concept Scale, Food Choice Inventory, and Eating Awareness Inventory indicated that self-concept scores were associated with vault scores, r(32) = .30, p < .042, and with the number of high nutrient foods eaten, r(54) = .25, p < .031. Group means between low, middle, and high scoring groups on five gymnastic events (vault, uneven bars, balance beam, floor exercise, and all around) showed significant differences between groups on the number of competitions attended by parents of vault performers, p < .0331, the number of high nutrient foods eaten by all-around performers, p < .0583, and the number of low nutrient foods and total foods eaten by balance beam performers, p < .0325 and p < .0343, respectively. Post-hoc tests revealed differences between low, middle, and high scoring groups. Significant differences in eating satisfaction and weight satisfaction were also found between performance groups. Implications emphasize the need to accentuate positive eating behaviors to influence gymnastic success and the need for development of nutrition education programs to foster positive eating behaviors among gymnasts.

Researchers have found that athletes, among them gymnasts, may be more susceptible to eating disorders (Burckes-Miller & Black, 1988; Costar, 1983; Gustafson, 1989; Richards, 1983; Rosen, McKeag, Hough, & Curley, 1986). Eating disorders among athletes are a major concern because of the potential detrimental impact on athletic performance and, ultimately, success. However, this paper raises the issue of accentuating positive eating behaviors and attitudes that influence gymnastic performance rather than dwelling almost exclusively on negative eating disorders.

Gymnastic success can be defined from a psychological, behavioral, and physiological perspective. For example, self-concept, a psychological factor, and eating behavior, a behavioral factor, may help to explain success in the sport of gymnastics. Equally important are the relationships that may exist between self-concept and eating behavior, between self-concept and gymnastic success, and between eating behavior and gymnastic success. Coaches who understand the interdependence and synergism of these variables with other mental, physical, emotional, social, and spiritual variables (Eberst, 1984; Greenberg, 1985a) may be able to predict the success of their individual athletes and teams. Ultimately, coaches might help their gymnasts recognize and develop the factors predictive of success.

The first purpose of this study was to describe and explain the relationship between self-concept, eating behavior, and gymnastic success of female collegiate gymnasts from Big Ten Conference teams. A second purpose was to isolate extraneous variables that might contaminate the explanation of the dependent variable, gymnastic success. The final purpose was to predict how the two main independent variables, self-concept and eating behavior, along with other independent variables, would help explain and predict gymnastic success of Big Ten Conference gymnasts and teams.

Method

Subjects

The female gymnasts ($n = 56$) who volunteered to participate were between the ages of 17 and 23 years ($M = 19.43$). The class breakdowns were 30% freshmen, 30% sophomores, 20% juniors, and 20% seniors. Gymnasts had between 6 and 17 total years of gymnastic experience ($M = 11.63$) and between 5 and 16 years of competitive experience ($M = 9.55$). Twenty-three percent ($n = 13$) of the gymnasts started gymnastics at age 8 while others began as early as age 3 (2%) and as late as age 12 (5%). The gymnasts represented Michigan State University, The Ohio State University, University of Illinois, University of Iowa, The University of Michigan, and University of Minnesota. The University of Wisconsin declined to participate in the study. Purdue University, Northwestern University, and University of Indiana do not have women's gymnastic teams. Gymnasts who were listed on their team's official 1987–88 roster were eligible to participate in the study. These rosters were verified by the coaches before the study began. Each team consisted of 8 to 12 gymnasts.

Procedures

Once approval to conduct the study was granted by the Human Subjects Review Committee at The Ohio State University, the researcher wrote to the Big Ten athletic directors for their support, then telephoned the Big Ten gymnastic coaches to determine their interest in the research project. Between Thanksgiving and Christmas, 1987, each of the six Big Ten Gymnastic coaches was sent a package containing a cover letter to the coach, an oral script for the research proctor, and a Research Testing Packet (RTP) for each gymnast.

Questionnaires

Each RTP held four paper-and-pencil questionnaires, which were administered in the following order: (a) Collegiate Gymnastics Profile, (b) Tennessee Self-Concept Scale, (c) Food Choice Inventory, and (d) Eating Awareness Inventory.

Collegiate Gymnastics Profile (CGP). The CGP was developed by Ubbes (1988) following the guidelines of Babbie (1979), Berdie and Anderson (1974), and Dillman (1978). The CGP (see Appendix 10.A) was designed to obtain information on gymnastic training practices, eating behaviors, eating disorders, health status, injury status, and family demographics. The questionnaire takes approximately five to seven minutes to complete.

Tennessee Self-Concept Scale (TSCS). Fitts (1964) developed the TSCS as a standardized, multidimensional scale to assess self-concept. The test has been used in over 582 research studies (Buros, 1978).[1] The TSCS requires subjects to rate themselves from one (completely false) to five (completely true) on 100 descriptive items related to low and high self-concept. Scores from the 100 items are summed to derive a Total Positive Score (TPS). Only the TPSs rather than any subscores

---

[1]In order to purchase and use the Tennessee Self Concept Scale, researchers must complete an application form listing educational and professional expertise. The TSCS Test Manual, the TSCS Counseling Form Test Booklet, and the TSCS Answer Sheet may be purchased from Western Psychological Services, 12031 Wilshire Boulevard, West Los Angeles, CA 90025; (213) 478-2061.

were used in this data analysis. The TPS measures a general level of self-concept, taking into account all aspects of self-concept. Fitts (1964) reported a test-retest reliability of .92 for the TPS with 60 college students over a two-week period. The instrument takes 10 to 20 minutes to complete.

Food Choice Inventory (FCI). The National Dairy Council (1985) developed the FCI for use with teenagers and adults. The FCI (see Appendix 10.B) contains a list of 25 high nutrient foods, 15 low nutrient foods, and 40 total foods. Subjects are instructed to identify foods from the 40-item list that they "will eat," "like but try not to eat," and "will not eat." Only the "will eat" data were analyzed for this study. The National Dairy Council found Cronbach alpha reliability coefficients for the "will eat" option of .81 for total foods, .77 for high nutrient foods, and .83 for low nutrient foods. In validation studies, an 85% agreement resulted between the FCI and actual food consumption. The inventory can be completed in two to three minutes.[2]

Eating Awareness Inventory (EAI). Richards (1983) developed the EAI (see Appendix 10.C) to describe when, where, with whom, how, and why (exclusive of physiological need) people eat. Only the "when" section (Part I) of the EAI was used for data analysis. In a field test with the EAI, Richards found that for Part I there was a 66.66% test-retest reliability and an internal consistency of .63 using Cronbach's alpha. The inventory can be completed in 5 to 10 minutes.[3]

Questionnaire Administration

The questionnaires were administered in December, 1987.[4] Prior to practice, coaches took teams to a classroom where a proctor read an oral script (see Appendix 10.D). Gymnasts were instructed to read the cover letters attached to their RTP before volunteering to participate in the study (see Appendix 10.E) All four questionnaires were completed in 35 to 50 minutes. Chewing gum was taped to the cover letter of each RTP based on the incentive benefit of such an approach reported by Miller and Smith (1983). In addition, gymnasts were encouraged to keep

---

[2]The Food Choice Inventory (manual and test) may be purchased from the National Dairy Council, 6300 North River Road, Rosemont, IL 60018-4233; (708) 696-1020.

[3]The revised version of the Eating Awareness Inventory for use with college students may be obtained from Jane E. Richards at University of Northern Iowa, School of Health, Physical Education and Leisure Studies, 203 West Gym, Cedar Falls, IA 50614-0241; (319) 273-3265.

[4]Directions for mailing the RTP were modified from feedback during a pilot study conducted with female collegiate gymnasts ($n = 11$) from Northern Illinois University in October 1987.

the pencil (supplied in the RTP) after completing their questionnaires. When finished, gymnasts were instructed by their cover letters to do the following: (a) return the questionnaires to their original manila envelope, (b) place their first and last names in the upper left corner of their mailing envelope (return address position), (c) remove the cover letter from the back of their envelope, and (d) secure the clasp and hand their sealed envelope to the proctor. All manila envelopes were then mailed directly to the researcher by the proctor. There was a 100% response rate which was verified by comparing names with team rosters.

Independent Variables

The primary independent variables were as follows: (a) self-concept and (b) eating behavior. The secondary independent variables were (a) class rank, (b) scholarship status (i.e., in-state athletic scholarship, out-of-state athletic scholarship, and nonscholarship, (c) birth order, and (d) university affiliation. The primary independent variables were measured by the TSCS and FCI, respectively. The secondary independent variables were measured by the CGP. Additional independent variables as identified by the CGP and the EAI were investigated.[5]

Dependent Variable

The dependent variable was gymnastic success as measured by seasonal average scores (SAS) on five different gymnastic events (vault, uneven bars, balance beam, floor exercise, and all around). Gymnasts compete on each event at least four times during the season to establish an SAS. Then, an average of four scores (two highest scores from "home" competitions and two highest scores from "away" competitions) are tallied for each gymnast and each team. Using SAS in this study provided greater confidence in the results compared to other studies that have defined success from one competition or championship only. The researcher received 1987–88 meet results in the mail each week from coaches and sports information directors for compilation of SAS. The SAS were cross-referenced with data from the four research questionnaires prior to analyses.

---

[5]Five variables related to gymnastics experience and training; two variables related to health and injury status; five variables related to eating behavior; four variables related to nutrition education; six variables related to body image; and one variable related to family demographics.

The 56 gymnasts were ranked and divided according to SAS into a lower one-third, middle one-third, and upper one-third scoring group on each gymnastic event. Consequently, group means were tested for significant differences on the five events for 30 independent variables.

Research Design

This study utilized an ex post facto research design to observe the dependent variable "first," then explain how the independent variables affect the dependent variable, and to investigate extraneous variables which might explain the dependent variable. Neither random selection nor random assignment of treatments could be used with this intact, homogeneous sample of collegiate gymnasts. Because alternative explanations in the form of extraneous variables were identified to explain the results, internal validity was not threatened.

Data Analysis

Descriptive statistics included measures of central tendency and Pearson product moment correlation. Inferential statistics included one-way analysis of variance and multiple regression analysis for normally distributed interval data. Nonparametric statistics included chi-squared for nominal data and Kruskal-Wallis one-way analysis of variance for skewed ordinal data (Hinkle, Wiersma, & Jurs, 1988).

Results

Results are organized by normative and statistical findings.

Normative Results

The CGP found that 25 gymnasts (44.6%) reported satisfaction with their eating habits, but 31 gymnasts (55.4%) reported dissatisfaction with their eating habits. Similarly, 26 gymnasts (46.4%) reported satisfaction with their body weight, but 30 gymnasts (53.6%) reported dissatisfaction with their body weight. When asked about their body fat, 21 gymnasts (38.9%) reported satisfaction, 31 gymnasts (57.4%) reported dissatisfaction, two gymnasts (3.7%) responded "would not like to admit," and two gymnasts (3.7%) chose not to respond.

When gymnasts were asked whether their teams participated in group nutrition education programs, 29 gymnasts (51.8%) reported "no," but 27 gymnasts (48.2%) reported "yes." Only one gymnastic team had a unanimous "yes" response. When gymnasts were asked from what source they obtained the most current nutrition information, responses included magazines and journals ($n = 20$), gymnastic team meetings ($n = 10$), home($n = 8$), food labels ($n = 6$), weight control programs ($n = 5$), formal college courses ($n = 4$), newspapers ($n = 1$), and television ($n = 1$). One gymnast reported no interest in nutrition. Gymnasts also reported a wide variety of people from whom they obtained the most current nutrition information. Responses included self ($n = 17$), gymnastic coach ($n = 9$), nutritionist ($n = 7$), gymnastic teammate ($n = 5$), parent ($n = 5$), college professor/instructor ($n = 4$), friend ($n = 4$), roommate ($n = 3$), registered dietitian ($n = 1$), and other family members besides parents ($n = 1$).

When asked how many times they ate meals during a typical week within the last month, results ranged from zero to seven times for breakfast and for lunch and from one to seven times for dinner. Only 27% ($n = 15$) of the gymnasts ate breakfast every day of the week. The next highest number of gymnasts ($n = 9$) ate breakfast only three days per week. Lunch was eaten every day of the week by 38% ($n = 21$) of the gymnasts. Eight gymnasts (14%) ate lunch at least five days per week, and another eight gymnasts (14%) ate lunch at least six days per week. Dinner was eaten every day of the week by 75% of the gymnasts ($n = 42$). Another 10% ($n = 6$) of the gymnasts ate dinner at least six days per week.

When asked the question "When did you eat your largest meal in the last month?" 57% ($n = 32$) of the gymnasts said in the evening; 18% ($n = 10$) indicated midday; and 7% ($n = 4$) specified morning; another 18% ($n = 10$) of the gymnasts ate equal amounts of food at breakfast, lunch, and dinner.

Statistical Results

Three Kruskal-Wallis one-way analyses of variance, seven one-way analyses of variance, twenty chi-squared statistics, and five multiple regression analyses were computed on variables for each of the five gymnastic events. Significant differences are presented by gymnastic event and summarized in Table 10.1.

Vault. In the vault event, a positive, moderate association, $r(32) = .30, p < .042$, was found between vault scores and self-concept

Table 10.1

Standardized Residuals for Low, Middle, and High Scoring Groups

Gymnastic Event	Questionnaire Response	Low Scoring Group	Middle Scoring Group	High Scoring Group
Vault	Satisfied with eating habits	-2.8 (n = 1)	1.6 (n = 7)	1.2 (n = 7)
	Dissatisfied with eating habits	2.8 (n = 10)	-1.6 (n = 4)	-1.2 (n = 5)
Floor Exercise	Satisfied with body weight	-2.2 (n = 2)	.4 (n = 5)	1.9 (n = 7)
	Dissatisfied with body weight	2.2 (n = 9)	-.4 (n = 5)	-1.9 (n = 3)
All Around	Satisfied with body weight	-2.9 (n = 0)	.5 (n = 3)	2.2 (n = 7)
	Dissatisfied with body weight	2.9 (n = 6)	-.5 (n = 2)	-2.2 (n = 2)

(TPS). A one-way analysis of variance (ANOVA) showed a significant difference on the number of competitions attended by parents between low ($n = 10$), middle ($n = 9$), and high scoring ($n = 12$) groups, $F(2, 28) = 3.86$, $p < .0331$. The critical value for a Tukey/Kramer post-hoc test (u) indicated that parents of high scoring vaulters attended significantly more competitions ($u_3 = 7$) than parents of low scoring vaulters ($u_1 = 2.7$), $u(2,28) = 3.5$, $p < .05$.

A chi-squared analysis showed a significant difference between vault groups on eating satisfaction, $X^2(2, N = 34) = 8.16$, $p < .0169$. Standardized residuals for the low scoring group contributed to the significant X^2 values. The majority (90%) of gymnasts ($n = 9$) in the low scoring group reported dissatisfaction with their eating habits, whereas in the high scoring group, 42% ($n = 5$) reported dissatisfaction. In the middle scoring group, only 36% ($n = 4$) reported dissatisfaction with their eating habits.

When four independent variables were entered into a multiple regression, 32.87% of the variance was explained. Self-concept (TPS), total years of gymnastic experience, number of high nutrient foods, and number of competitions that parents attended significantly predicted vault success, $F(4, 26) = 3.18$, $p < .0296$.

Uneven Bars. No significant differences between groups or significant predictors for bar success were found.

Balance Beam. In the beam event, a negative moderate association approached significance between beam scores and the number of low nutrient foods that gymnasts ate, $r(31) = -.28$, $p < .06$. Gymnasts who scored lower on balance beam preferred to eat more low nutrient foods, whereas gymnasts who scored higher on balance beam preferred to eat fewer low nutrient foods. A one-way analysis of variance showed a significant difference in the number of low nutrient foods eaten by gymnasts in the low ($n = 11$), middle ($n = 11$), and high ($n = 11$) scoring groups, $F(2,30) = 3.85$, $p < .0325$. The critical value for a Tukey post-hoc test indicated that the middle scoring group ($u_2 = 8.6$) preferred to eat significantly more low nutrient foods than the high scoring group ($u_3 = 3.8$), $u(2,30) = 3.49$, $p < .05$.

Another one-way analysis of variance showed a significant difference in the number of total foods eaten by gymnasts in the low ($n = 11$), middle ($n = 11$), and high ($n = 11$) scoring groups, $F(2, 30) = 3.78$, $p < .0343$. The critical value for a Tukey post-hoc test indicated that the middle scoring group ($u_2 = 23.64$) preferred to eat significantly more total foods than the high scoring group ($u_3 = 16.55$), $u(2,30) = 3.49$, $p < .05$.

A chi-squared analysis found that while groups were not significantly different on body fat satisfaction and team exposure to nutrition education, these variables approached significance, $X^2(2, N = 33) = 4.89, p < .0868$; $X^2(2, N = 33) = 5.13, p < .0768$, respectively.

Floor Exercise. A chi-squared analysis showed a significant difference in body weight satisfaction between the low, middle, and high scoring groups in the floor exercise event, $X^2(2, N = 31) = 5.82, p < .0545$. Standardized residuals for the low scoring group contributed to the significant X^2 values. Most gymnasts (82%) in the low scoring group ($n = 9$) were not satisfied with their body weight, whereas most gymnasts (70%) in the high scoring group ($n = 7$) were satisfied with their body weight. Body weight satisfaction in the middle scoring group was equally distributed between 50% ($n = 5$) "yes" responses and 50% ($n = 5$) "no" responses.

All Around. A chi-squared analysis showed a significant difference in body weight satisfaction for the all around groups, $X^2(2, N = 21) = 8.98, p < .0112)$. Standardized residuals for the low and high scoring groups contributed to the significant X^2 values. All of the gymnasts in the low scoring group ($n = 6$) were not satisfied with their body weight, whereas most gymnasts (78%) in the high scoring group ($n = 7$) were satisfied with their body weight. Body weight satisfaction in the middle scoring group was 60% ($n = 3$) for "yes" responses and 40% ($n = 2$) for "no" responses.

A one-way analysis of variance showed a significant difference in the number of high nutrient foods eaten by gymnasts in the low ($n = 6$), middle ($n = 5$), and high ($n = 9$) scoring groups, $F(2, 17) = 3.37, p < .0583$. The critical value for a Tukey/Kramer post-hoc test indicated that the middle scoring group ($u_2 = 9.8$) preferred to eat significantly fewer high nutrient foods than the high scoring group ($u_3 = 15$), $u(2,17) = 3.63, p < .05$.

Discussion

A positive approach to characterizing healthy, successful gymnasts is glaringly absent in gymnastics research. Instead, interventions have a *problem* theme. A suggested rationale for choosing this approach may be based on the probable assumption that if some gymnasts have eating disorders then most gymnasts have eating disorders. This study focuses on a broader issue. Should coaches spend time and effort identifying gymnasts with eating pathologies or should they identify and encourage gymnasts who practice more positive eating behaviors? While eating disorders may be problematic for gymnasts in search of peak performance, it is important not to lose sight of other gymnasts who are also in search of peak performance. The tendency to dwell on eating problems to the exclusion of a broader, holistic picture may be too narrow. There are some gymnasts who practice healthful eating behaviors and need to be encouraged to maintain their positive behaviors, and other gymnasts who might improve their eating behaviors if they were guided in a positive way by exemplary role models.

Research has concluded that athletes need exposure to health education with a focus on proper nutrition, weight loss management, body image, exemplary role models, and goal setting strategies (Black & Burckes-Miller, 1988; Eisenman, 1990; Linsdey & Janz, 1985). However, other research suggests that some coaches lack training in how to help athletes in the basics of good nutrition (Cohen, Tokarcyzk, & Zylks, 1989; Parr, Porter, & Hodgson, 1984).

Educational workshops or mini-training sessions with team members might be developed to improve knowledge, attitudes, and behaviors about sport nutrition. Coaches and gymnasts who practice healthful eating behaviors could serve as exemplary role models to other team members who receive inaccurate nutrition information and/or practice poor eating behaviors. Too often, healthy gymnasts are obstructed from serving as role models to other gymnasts because of individual jealousies, team competitiveness, peer pressure, and lack of positive support from their coaches. Coaches and gymnasts should recognize and understand how interpersonal relationships and environmental factors influence eating behavior. This may mean that coaches should first help gymnasts to identify personal health needs and then work together on strategies to meet those needs (Greenberg, 1985b).

For the most part, nutrition education is a missing component in the majority of gymnastic training programs. In the current study, only one out of six gymnastic teams unanimously reported an involvement in organized nutrition education sessions. However, one-half of the gymnasts indicated that their teams participated in group nutrition education programs. This discrepancy may be explained by the extent of the educational programs. Perhaps only the one team had consistent exposure to sport nutrition on a regular basis during the precompetitive season.

The two major independent variables in this study were self-concept and eating behavior. Self-concept and eating behavior are thought to be components of gymnastic success, yet the actual relationships between them are generally not reported in the literature. For female collegiate gymnasts in the Big Ten Conference, a positive relationship existed between self-concept and high nutrient foods. Thus, gymnasts with higher self-concepts tended to have better eating behaviors, whereas gymnasts with lower self-concepts tended to have poorer eating behaviors.

An important priority for future research is the clarification of the role that eating behavior plays in gymnastic success. Studies might be designed to determine whether any significant differences exist between male and female gymnasts at colleges, high schools, and private clubs. In this study, low scoring gymnasts on balance beam ate more high fat junk foods than high scoring gymnasts. In the all-around event, high scoring gymnasts ate more high nutrient foods than middle scoring gymnasts. Thus, healthful food choices seem to make a difference in successful performances.

Comparison of this study to another study of eating behaviors shows that college gymnasts are similar to other college students. Parsons (1985) found that two-thirds of the college students studied did not eat breakfast or lunch on a consistent basis, but a majority of respondents ate an evening meal. Two-thirds of the collegiate gymnasts in the current study did not eat breakfast or lunch either, but slightly more gymnasts than college students ate their largest meal at midday. This may highlight the positive eating behaviors of some of the gymnasts who understand the need for adequate nutrition for afternoon workouts. Nevertheless, a majority of gymnasts ate their largest meal in the evening. Further research is needed to determine how energy utilization, eating behavior, and successful performance are related.

This study also found that low scoring gymnasts on floor exercise and all around were not as satisfied with their body weights as high scoring gymnasts. And in the vault event, low scoring gymnasts were not as satisfied with their eating habits as middle and high scoring gymnasts. Consequently, the goals of an educational program in these areas might be directed toward identifying healthier gymnasts as role models and moving less healthy gymnasts toward better health.

In conclusion, this study emphasizes the need to focus on building and developing positive eating behaviors among gymnasts rather than just preventing and treating negative eating disorders. Failure to implement nutrition education programs that are grounded in health promotion may lead to an overemphasis on treatment for a few gymnasts and may send the wrong messages to healthy gymnasts. There is a need to educate all gymnasts on the role of positive eating behaviors in successful performance. The implications of developing healthier eating behaviors among gymnasts remain to be seen. If factors leading to successful performance can be identified, a positive approach can be implemented rather than one that focuses solely on problem behaviors.

References

Babbie, E. R. (1979). *The practice of social research* (2nd ed.). Belmont, CA: Wadsworth Publishing Company.

Berdie, D. R., & Anderson, J. F. (1974). *Questionnaires: Design and use.* Metuchen, NJ: Scarecrow Press.

Black, D. R., & Burckes-Miller, M. E. (1988). Male and female college athletes: Use of anorexia nervosa and bulimia nervosa weight loss methods. *Research Quarterly for Exercise and Sport, 59,* 252–256.

Burckes-Miller, M. E., & Black, D. R. (1988). Male and female college athletes: Prevalence of anorexia nervosa and bulimia nervosa. *Athletic Training, 23,* 137–140.

Buros, O. K. (1978). *The eighth mental measurements yearbook.* Highland Park, NJ: The Gryphon Press.

Cohen, C. J., Tokarczyk, C. R., & Zylks, D. R. (1989). Nutrition knowledge and practice of university athletes, coaches, and student athletic trainers. *Illinois Journal of Health, Physical Education, Recreation and Dance, 26,* 10–11.

Costar, E. D., (1983). Eating disorders: Gymnasts at risk. *International Gymnast, 25*(11), 58–59.

Dillman, D. A. (1978). *Mail and telephone surveys: Total design method.* New York: John Wiley & Sons.

Eberst, R. M. (1984). Defining health: A multidimensional model. *Journal of School Health, 54,* 99–104.

Eisenman, P. (1990). Nutritional safety. In J. S. George (Ed.), *United States Gymnastics Federation Safety Manual* (2nd ed.). Indianapolis, IN: USGF Publications.

Fitts, W. H. (1964). *Tennessee self-concept scale.* Los Angeles: Western Psychological Services.

Greenberg, J. S. (1985a). Health and wellness: A conceptual differentiation. *Journal of School Health, 55,* 403–406.

Greenberg, J. S. (1985b). Iatrogenic health education disease. *Health Education, 16*(5), 4–6.

Gustafson, D. (1989). Eating behaviors of women college athletes. *Melpomene Journal, 8,* 11–13.

Hinkle, D. E., Wiersma, W., & Jurs, S. G. (1988). *Applied statistics for the behavioral sciences* (2nd ed.). Boston: Houghton Mifflin Company.

Lindsey, B. J., & Janz, K. F. (1985). A healthy connection: Helping physical educators address eating disorders. *Journal of Physical Education, Recreation and Dance, 56*(9), 41–44.

Miller, L. E., & Smith, K. L. (1983, September/October). Handling nonresponse issues. *Journal of Extension, 21,* 45–50.

National Dairy Council. (1985). *Food choice inventory*. Rosemont, IL: National Dairy Council and University of Illinois at Chicago.

Parr, R. B., Porter, M. A., & Hodgson, S. C. (1984). Nutrition knowledge and practice of coaches, trainers, and athletes. *The Physician and Sportsmedicine, 12*(3), 126–138.

Parsons, N. P. (1985). *A description of eating practices of selected university students*. (Unpublished master's thesis, Southern Illinois University, Carbondale).

Richards, J. E. (1983). Development of an eating awareness inventory and its use among university faculty and administrators. (Doctoral dissertation, Southern Illinois University at Carbondale, 1982). *Dissertation Abstracts International, 43*, 2245–46A.

Rosen, L. W., McKeag, D. B., Hough, D. O., & Curley, V. (1986). Pathogenic weight control behavior in female athletes. *The Physician and Sportsmedicine, 14*(1), 79–86.

Ubbes, V. A. (1989). Relationship between self concept, eating behavior, and gymnastic success of female collegiate gymnasts from Big Ten Conference teams. (Doctoral dissertation, The Ohio State University, 1988). *Dissertation Abstracts International, 50*, 633–A.

Author Notes

The author thanks Brent E. Wholeben and his associates at the Office of Research, Evaluation, and Policy Studies at Northern Illinois University for their assistance with the statistics, and David R. Black of Purdue University for his invaluable assistance in the preparation of this manuscript.

Appendix 10.A

COLLEGIATE GYMNASTICS PROFILE

DIRECTIONS: Please answer each item as honestly as possible by circling the letter of the best response or by filling in the blank. If unsure about a question, make an educated guess. Do not leave any items blank.

1. Name of your school:

   1. UNIVERSITY OF ILLINOIS
   2. UNIVERSITY OF IOWA
   3. UNIVERSITY OF MICHIGAN
   4. MICHIGAN STATE UNIVERSITY
   5. UNIVERSITY OF MINNESOTA
   6. OHIO STATE UNIVERSITY
   7. UNIVERSITY OF WISCONSIN

2. Current year in school:

   1. FRESHMAN
   2. SOPHOMORE
   3. JUNIOR
   4. SENIOR

3. Your age: _____ YEARS

4. Number of brothers and sisters in your family
   (not including yourself):   _____ SIBLINGS

5. Your birth order:

   1. FIRST BORN
   2. MIDDLE BORN, NOT FIRST BORN OR LAST BORN
   3. LAST BORN
   4. ONLY CHILD

6. Your family status:

   1. PARENTS MARRIED; TOGETHER
   2. PARENTS APART; LIVING WITH MOTHER
   3. PARENTS APART; LIVING WITH FATHER
   4. FATHER DECEASED; LIVING WITH MOTHER
   5. MOTHER DECEASED; LIVING WITH FATHER
   6. OTHER

7. Your parents' combined estimated yearly earnings:

   1. LESS THAN $10,000   6. $50,000 TO 59,999
   2. $10,000 TO 19,999   7. $60,000 TO 69,999
   3. $20,000 TO 29,999   8. MORE THAN $69,999
   4. $30,000 TO 39,999   9. WOULD NOT LIKE TO ADMIT
   5. $40,000 TO 49,999   10. HAVE NO IDEA

Continued on next page

8. How is your education being financed? (Circle as many as apply)

    1. PAYING FOR SCHOOL YOURSELF
    2. PARENT(S) PAYING FOR SCHOOL
    3. LOAN
    4. GRANT
    5. ACADEMIC SCHOLARSHIP
    6. GIFT FROM FAMILY OR FRIEND
    7. FOUR-YEAR ATHLETIC SCHOLARSHIP

9. Your athletic status:

    1. IN-STATE SCHOLARSHIP ATHLETE
    2. OUT-OF-STATE SCHOLARSHIP ATHLETE
    3. NONSCHOLARSHIP ATHLETE

10. At the present time, do you have an injury that would limit your ability to compete:

    1. YES
    2. NO

11. Other than any injuries, how would you rate your current health status from a mental and physical perspective:

    1. EXCELLENT HEALTH STATUS
    2. GOOD HEALTH STATUS
    3. AVERAGE HEALTH STATUS
    4. FAIR HEALTH STATUS
    5. POOR HEALTH STATUS

12. Age when you took your first gymnastics lessons or training:
    _____ YEARS

13. Number of training months per year in gymnastics: _____ MONTHS

14. Years of participation in competitive gymnastics: _____ YEARS

15. Total years of participation in gymnastics, including competitive gymnastics: _____ YEARS

16. Number of competitions per season attended by one or both parents:
    _____ MEETS

17. Number of competitions per season attended by close friend (either sex):   _____ MEETS

18. From what one source do you obtain the most current information about nutrition:

   1. PERSONAL READING OF MAGAZINES/JOURNALS
   2. PERSONAL READING OF NEWSPAPERS
   3. GYMNASTICS TEAM MEETINGS
   4. RADIO
   5. TELEVISION
   6. WEIGHT CONTROL PROGRAMS
   7. HEALTH FOOD STORES
   8. FOOD LABELS
   9. FORMAL COLLEGE COURSES
  10. HOME
  11. NOT INTERESTED IN NUTRITION

19. From whom do you obtain the most current information about nutrition:

   1. YOURSELF
   2. GYMNASTICS COACH
   3. GYMNASTICS TEAMMATE
   4. ROOMMATE
   5. FRIEND
   6. PARENT
   7. COLLEGE INSTRUCTOR/PROFESSOR
   8. NUTRITIONIST
   9. REGISTERED DIETITIAN
  10. OTHER FAMILY MEMBERS BESIDES PARENTS

20. How would you rate your interest in nutrition and food awareness?

   1. VERY INTERESTED
   2. MILDLY INTERESTED
   3. NO INTEREST

21. Has your gymnastics team participated in nutrition education sessions as a collective group:

   1. YES
   2. NO
   3. WOULD NOT LIKE TO ADMIT

22. Have you ever sought professional help for symptoms of overweight:

   1. YES
   2. NO
   3. WOULD NOT LIKE TO ADMIT

23. Have you ever sought professional help for symptoms of anorexia nervosa:

   1. YES
   2. NO
   3. WOULD NOT LIKE TO ADMIT

24. Have you ever sought professional help for symptoms of bulimia:
    1. YES
    2. NO
    3. WOULD NOT LIKE TO ADMIT

25. Have you ever been medically diagnosed and treated for any eating disorder or problem:
    1. YES
    2. NO
    3. WOULD NOT LIKE TO ADMIT

26. Are you satisfied with your eating habits:
    1. YES
    2. NO
    3. WOULD NOT LIKE TO ADMIT

27. Are you satisfied with your body weight:
    1. YES
    2. NO
    3. WOULD NOT LIKE TO ADMIT

28. Are you satisfied with your percent body fat:
    1. YES
    2. NO
    3. WOULD NOT LIKE TO ADMIT

Appendix 10.B

Food Choice Inventory

We all like some foods and dislike other foods. There is nothing "good" or "bad" about this.

Using the list of 40 foods on the next page, you are asked to identify your food choices. You have probably eaten many of the foods. Some of the foods in the list you may never have tasted.

Directions

First look at the two examples below. There are three ways to respond. SELECT:

A = if you WILL EAT the food
B = if you LIKE BUT TRY NOT TO EAT the food too often
C = if you WILL NOT EAT the food

Circle the letter that best indicates your food choice. For example, if you like granola, then you would circle A as shown below. Now circle the letter that best describes your choice for the second example, beets.

Example

	WILL EAT A	LIKE BUT TRY NOT TO EAT B	WILL NOT EAT C
GRANOLA	(A)	B	C
BEETS	A	B	C

When you are clear about how to respond, you are ready to begin marking your choices on the 40 item food list. The instructor will tell you when to begin.

	WILL EAT A	LIKE BUT TRY NOT TO EAT B	WILL NOT EAT C
1. APPLE PIE	A	B	C
2. BEAN SPROUTS	A	B	C
3. BLACKEYED PEAS	A	B	C
4. BROCCOLI	A	B	C
5. BUTTER	A	B	C
6. CANDY	A	B	C
7. CANNOLI	A	B	C
8. CAULIFLOWER	A	B	C
9. CHICKEN	A	B	C
10. COOKED GREENS	A	B	C
11. COOKIES	A	B	C
12. CORN CHIPS	A	B	C
13. COTTAGE CHEESE	A	B	C
14. DONUTS	A	B	C
15. EGG ROLL	A	B	C
16. EGGS	A	B	C
17. FISH	A	B	C
18. FRENCH DRESSING	A	B	C
19. GELATIN CUBES	A	B	C
20. GRITS	A	B	C
21. GYROS	A	B	C
22. HAMBURGER PATTY	A	B	C
23. HAM HOCKS	A	B	C
24. JAM	A	B	C
25. KALE	A	B	C
26. LIVER PATÉ	A	B	C
27. LOW FAT MILK	A	B	C
28. MARGARINE	A	B	C
29. OATMEAL	A	B	C
30. OYSTERS	A	B	C
31. POTATO CHIPS	A	B	C
32. QUICHE	A	B	C
33. SOFT DRINK	A	B	C
34. SKIM MILK	A	B	C
35. SPICE CAKE	A	B	C
36. SWEET ROLL	A	B	C
37. WHITE BREAD	A	B	C
38. WHOLE MILK	A	B	C
39. WHOLE WHEAT BREAD	A	B	C
40. YOGURT	A	B	C

For office use only   T

H

L

List of 25 HIGH and 15 LOW Nutrient-Value Food Items*

HIGH Nutrient-Value Foods	LOW Nutrient-Value Foods
2. bean sprouts	1. apple pie
3. blackeyed peas	5. butter
4. broccoli	6. candy
8. cauliflower	7. cannoli
9. chicken	11. cookies
10. cooked greens	12. corn chips
13. cottage cheese	14. donuts
15. egg roll	18. French dressing
16. eggs	19. gelatin cubes
17. fish	24. jam
20. grits	28. margarine
21. gyros	31. potato chips
22. hamburger patty	33. soft drink
23. ham hocks	35. spice cake
25. kale	36. sweet roll
26. liver paté	
27. lowfat milk	*The criterion for classifying foods into
29. oatmeal	high and low nutrient-value foods is based on
30. oysters	a comparison of the percentage of the U.S.
32. quiche	Recommended Daily Allowances for any one
34. skim milk	of the eight leader nutrients and the percent-
37. white bread	age of the allowance for calories in a serving
38. whole milk	of the food. If the nutrient "value" is higher
39. whole wheat bread	than the caloric "value," the food is desig-
40. yogurt	nated as a high nutrient-value food.

**The Nine Scales in the *Food Choice Inventory:*
What Each Describes**

	A	B	C
T	Foods from the total list of 40 one WILL EAT	Foods from the total list of 40 one will LIKE BUT TRY NOT TO EAT	Foods from the total list of 40 one WILL NOT EAT
H	Foods from the 25 high in nutrient value one WILL EAT	Foods from the 25 high in nutrient value one will LIKE BUT TRY NOT TO EAT	Foods from the 25 high in nutrient value one WILL NOT EAT
L	Foods from the 15 low in nutrient value one WILL EAT	Foods from the 15 low in nutrient value one will LIKE BUT TRY NOT TO EAT	Foods from the 15 low in nutrient value one WILL NOT EAT

Appendix 10.C

EATING AWARENESS INVENTORY
An instrument to describe selected eating practices
—When, Where, With Whom, How, Why—

Copyrighted by
Jane E. Richards, Ph.D.
Division of Health
School of Health, Physical Education and Recreation
University of Northern Iowa

Instructions for Respondents

This inventory is designed to describe five selected eating practices—WHEN, WHERE, WITH WHOM, HOW, and WHY you eat. There are no correct or incorrect answers. Please read each item carefully and choose the response(s) that reflect most closely YOUR PERSONAL eating practices. Your name is not required. Responses will be analyzed for the group as a whole. Please answer *all* of the items.

THANK YOU!

EAI PART I—WHEN?

For items 1 and 2 below, check (✔) the *one* response which indicates THE NUMBER OF TIMES, during a typical week within the past month, when you ate the specified meals and snacks.

*Number of Times Eaten
in a Typical Week*

	0	1	2	3	4	5	6	7
1. MEAL*								
(a) morning meal	☐	☐	☐	☐	☐	☐	☐	☐
(b) midday meal	☐	☐	☐	☐	☐	☐	☐	☐
(c) evening meal	☐	☐	☐	☐	☐	☐	☐	☐
2. SNACK**								
(a) mid-morning snack	☐	☐	☐	☐	☐	☐	☐	☐
(b) mid-afternoon snack	☐	☐	☐	☐	☐	☐	☐	☐
(c) early evening snack	☐	☐	☐	☐	☐	☐	☐	☐
(d) late evening snack	☐	☐	☐	☐	☐	☐	☐	☐

*MEAL refers to one of the regular occasions during a day when food is taken.
**SNACK refers to food eaten between regular meals.

For items 3–9 below, check (✔) the *one* response which best describes your eating practices during the past month.

	Never	Seldom	Some-times	Often	Always

DID YOU . . . .

3. eat *more* than three meals per day (exclusive of snacking)?

4. eat when you were not busy?

5. eat *meals* when you were not hungry?

6. eat *snacks* when you were not hungry?

7. eat while you were talking on the telephone?

8. (a) watch television while you were eating *meals*?

   (b) read while you were eating *meals*?

   (c) conduct business, study, or work while you were eating *meals*?

9. (a) eat *snacks* while you were watching television?

   (b) eat *snacks* while you were reading?

   (c) eat *snacks* while you were conducting business, studying, or working?

For items 10–12 below, check (✔) the *one* response which best describes your eating practices during the past month.

10. Which of the following best describes your eating practices on weekends as compared to weekdays?

    (a) I tended to eat *more* on weekends, less on weekdays
    (b) I tended to eat *less* on weekends, more on weekdays
    (c) I tended to eat about the *same* on weekends as on weekdays

11. When did you eat the MAJORITY of your *snacks*?

☐ (a) mid-morning
☐ (b) mid-afternoon
☐ (c) early evening
☐ (d) late evening
☐ (e) I did not eat snacks

12. When did you eat your LARGEST *meal*?

☐ (a) morning
☐ (b) midday
☐ (c) evening
☐ (d) I ate about the same at all meals
☐ (e) I snacked throughout the day rather than eating meals

EAI PART II—WHERE?

NOTE: Item 1 below is NOT concerned with the place where you ate, but rather, the *SOURCE* from where you obtained the food you ate. For each of the three meals listed, enter THE NUMBER OF TIMES, during a typical week within the past month, that a given meal was obtained from the *SOURCES* specified. (The horizontal total for each meal should equal 7.)

1. MEAL	Prepaid University Food Service (e.g., Residence Hall Cafeteria)	Own residence (e.g., home, apartment, etc.)	Residence of friend or relative	Restaurant: carry out, drive-thru & cafeteria/self-service	Restaurant: Table Service	Vending Machine	Did not eat	Other, please specify
(a) morning meal								
(b) midday meal								
(c) evening meal								

For items 2–4 below, check (✔) the *one* response which best describes your eating practices during the past month.

DID YOU . . .	Never	Seldom	Some-times	Often	Always	Does not Apply
2. eat snacks at parties and other similar social events?	☐	☐	☐	☐	☐	☐
3. eat snacks at movies, sporting events, concerts, etc.?	☐	☐	☐	☐	☐	☐
4. (a) eat *meals* while driving or riding in a car or other motor vehicle?	☐	☐	☐	☐	☐	☐
(b) eat *snacks* while driving or riding in a car or other motor vehicle?	☐	☐	☐	☐	☐	☐

EAI PART III—WITH WHOM?

For each of the three meals listed in item 1 below, check (✔) the *one* response which best describes WITH WHOM, during the past month, you usually ate a given meal.

1. MEAL	Alone	With persons sharing your residence	With relatives not living at your residence	With friends not living at your residence	Did not eat	Other, please specify
(a) morning meal	☐	☐	☐	☐	☐	_____
(b) midday meal	☐	☐	☐	☐	☐	_____
(c) evening meal	☐	☐	☐	☐	☐	_____

2. During the past month, which *one* of the following best describes the AMOUNT of food you ate when you were eating alone as compared to when you were eating with others?

☐ (a) I tended to eat *more* when I was alone than when I was with others
☐ (b) I tended to eat *less* when I was alone than when I was with others
☐ (c) I tended to eat about the *same* when I was alone and when I was with others
☐ (d) I did not eat alone
☐ (e) I did not eat with others

EAI PART IV—HOW?

For items 1–10 below, check (✔) the *one* response which best describes your eating practices during the past month.

	Never	Seldom	Some-times	Often	Always
DID YOU . . .					
1. eat until you felt full?	☐	☐	☐	☐	☐
2. continue to eat after you felt full?	☐	☐	☐	☐	☐
3. eat very fast without really chewing your food?	☐	☐	☐	☐	☐
4. eat slowly and leisurely?	☐	☐	☐	☐	☐
5. have periods when you ate very little, i.e., much less than you normally eat?	☐	☐	☐	☐	☐
6. have periods when you ate a great deal, i.e., much more than you normally eat?	☐	☐	☐	☐	☐
7. sit at a table when you ate meals?	☐	☐	☐	☐	☐
8. linger at the table or other setting after eating a meal?	☐	☐	☐	☐	☐
9. eat in secrecy?	☐	☐	☐	☐	☐
10. eat or "nibble" unconsciously without really being aware that you were eating?	☐	☐	☐	☐	☐

EAT PART V—WHY?

For items 1–22 which follow, check (✔) the *one* response which best describes your eating practices during the past month.

WHEN I WAS . . .	I did not eat	I ate less than I usually eat	I ate the same as I usually eat	I ate more than I usually eat	I did not experience this condition
1. tired and fatigued	☐	☐	☐	☐	☐
2. anxious, tense, and nervous	☐	☐	☐	☐	☐
3. calm and relaxed	☐	☐	☐	☐	☐
4. frightened	☐	☐	☐	☐	☐
5. bored	☐	☐	☐	☐	☐
6. angry	☐	☐	☐	☐	☐
7. in a stressful situation	☐	☐	☐	☐	☐
8. happy	☐	☐	☐	☐	☐
9. upset	☐	☐	☐	☐	☐
10. proud of an achievement	☐	☐	☐	☐	☐
11. criticized for lack of achievement	☐	☐	☐	☐	☐
12. depressed	☐	☐	☐	☐	☐
13. relieved that an unpleasant situation was over	☐	☐	☐	☐	☐
14. confident and self-assured	☐	☐	☐	☐	☐
15. feeling guilty	☐	☐	☐	☐	☐
16. short-tempered and irritable	☐	☐	☐	☐	☐
17. lonely	☐	☐	☐	☐	☐
18. sad	☐	☐	☐	☐	☐

	Never	Seldom	Some-times	Often	Always
19. feeling rejected	☐	☐	☐	☐	☐
20. praised and com-plimented	☐	☐	☐	☐	☐
21. frustrated	☐	☐	☐	☐	☐
22. insecure and uncertain	☐	☐	☐	☐	☐

For items 23–30 below, check (✔) the *one* response which best describes your eating practices during the past month.

DID YOU . . .	Never	Seldom	Some-times	Often	Always
23. reward yourself by eating?	☐	☐	☐	☐	☐
24. eat to perk yourself up or give yourself a lift?	☐	☐	☐	☐	☐
25. eat because you liked the taste of food in your mouth?	☐	☐	☐	☐	☐
26. "celebrate" an important event or day by eating in a special way?	☐	☐	☐	☐	☐
27. eat to be polite and sociable even if you were not hungry?	☐	☐	☐	☐	☐
28. eat for pleasure and enjoyment?	☐	☐	☐	☐	☐
29. eat because it was your regularly scheduled mealtime even if you were not hungry?	☐	☐	☐	☐	☐
30. eat in response to: (a) watching other people eat?	☐	☐	☐	☐	☐
(b) viewing a food commerical on television?	☐	☐	☐	☐	☐
(c) seeing a food advertisement in a magazine or newspaper?	☐	☐	☐	☐	☐
(d) the smell or sight of food?	☐	☐	☐	☐	☐

Appendix 10.D

Oral Script for Research Proctor

(Please read this script to the gymnasts at the beginning of the testing session.)

Valerie Striggow-Ubbes, a Ph.D. candidate at Ohio State, has asked you to participate in her study entitled "The Relationship between Self-Concept, Eating Behavior, and Gymnastics Success of Female Collegiate Gymnasts from NCAA Big Ten Conference Teams." All female gymnasts in the Big Ten have been asked to participate in this study. You will be asked to answer questions ranging from your gymnastics training to your eating habits.

Your participation in this study is strictly on a volunteer basis. You may decline to participate at any time during the survey session. All information on these questionnaires will be completely confidential. You will be asked to place your name on the sealed envelope AFTER you complete the questionnaires. Your name is needed so that your Seasonal Average Scores on the vault, uneven bars, balance beam, and floor exercise can be matched to your questionnaires at the end of the season. Once matching occurs, your name will be anonymous again. All participants will be analyzed as a group. No individual results will be determined.

As soon as I finish reading this, you will be given a manila envelope containing the survey questionnaires. A cover letter will be attached to the envelope. The letter will have a piece of chewing gum taped to it. You may keep the chewing gum even if you choose not to participate. After reading the cover letter, open your envelope, and remove the four questionnaires. There is a pencil in the envelope for filling out the questionnaires. You may keep the pencil, too. Read the directions for each of the questionnaires before you answer any of the questions for that questionnaire. Please answer all of the questions without leaving any answers blank. Do not talk to anyone during the survey session. If you do not understand an item on a questionnaire, reread the directions for that questionnaire. If you are still not sure about your answer to a question, make the best guess you can. Even though one of the questionnaires has a space for your name, do not put your name on any of the questionnaires.

The surveys should take about thirty-five minutes to complete. After you have finished, put the completed questionnaires into the original envelope. Even if you have decided not to participate, place the uncompleted questionnaires into the original envelope. Seal the envelope. Print your first and last name in the return address portion of the envelope where indicated. Return the sealed envelope to the person who gave it to you. These instructions are repeated for you in the cover letter.

(Distribute the envelopes)

Please take a moment to read the cover letter attached to your manila envelope.

Appendix 10.E

Cover Letter to Gymnasts in Research Testing Packet

Dear Big Ten Gymnast:

I am a Ph.D. candidate in Health Education at The Ohio State University. From 1983 to 1986, I served as the Assistant Coach of Women's Gymnastics at OSU. I am currently writing my dissertation on the topic of self concept, eating behaviors, and gymnastics success. My research is under the jurisdiction of my advisor, Dr. Mary K. Beyrer. The purpose of this letter is to request your involvement in my study.

Your participation in this study is strictly on a volunteer basis. Should you agree to participate, you will spend the next thirty-five minutes answering four questionnaires. Your responses will be completely confidential. Your name is needed on the outside of the original envelope so that your Seasonal Average Scores can be matched to your responses at the end of your gymnastics season. Once matching occurs, your name will be anonymous again. No individual results will be reported in my final dissertation.

Attached to this letter is a manila envelope containing the questionnaires which will ask you various questions about your gymnastics training, your family, and your eating practices. Please read the directions for each questionnaire before you answer any of the questions on that questionnaire. Once you begin the questionnaire(s), it is imperative that you answer every question. Please do not leave any answers blank. However if you feel uncomfortable with any question, you do not have to answer it. Should you be unsure about your response, make an "educated guess." Work through the questions quickly without talking to your teammates or coaches.

PLEASE FOLLOW THESE STEPS WHETHER OR NOT YOU CHOOSE
TO PARTICIPATE:

1. Put your completed (or uncompleted) questionnaires back into the original envelope and seal it.
2. Place your full name in the upper left hand corner of the same side of the envelope that has the postage. Your name should not appear on any of the questionnaires.
3. Remove this letter from the outside of the envelope and discard it.
4. Return the sealed envelope to the same person who gave it to you.

I thank you in advance for your participation in my study. I hope you will find the experience worthwhile, knowing that you have contributed to research in our great sport of gymnastics.

Sincerely,

Valerie Striggow-Ubbes

P.S. Enjoy this chewing gum while you complete the questionnaires. You may also keep the pencil when you are finished.

11

Eating Disorders Among Athletes: The Future

DAVID R. BLACK

The purpose of this chapter is to suggest an option for organizing future research and service activities related to eating disorders and athletes. A national task force or consortium is proposed modeled after the Surgeon General's health objectives for the nation. Sponsoring organizations or agencies are suggested as well as disciplines that might provide leadership. Four general topic areas are offered and examples of issues to be addressed are provided. The final outcome of such a task force would be the development of measurable objectives for the nation related to eating disorders and athletes. The coordinated broad scale effort is suggested to supply an organized approach to meet the challenge of abating a serious problem in sport.

Athletes experience many stresses in our society and display a wide variety of social problems. Too many athletes are involved in some type of abuse or a behavior carried to extreme (obsessive compulsive disorders). Some of these abuses and extremes include alcohol, drugs (e.g., steroids), gambling, and eating disorders. Collectively, these difficulties suggest that societal standards and expectations as well as the sport environment, in particular, should serve as topics for debate and value clarification. In addition to research and ongoing service activities, a large scale coordinated effort is needed to diminish or abate the frequency of eating disorders in athletics as well as the occurrence of other social-psychological problems.

Exemplar of a National Task Force

One action that might be taken is to organize a national task force or consortium to focus on eating disorders among athletes. Perhaps one of the better known examples was initiated in 1979 with the publication of *Healthy People: The Surgeon General's Report on Health Promotion and Disease Prevention.* Based on that document, a task force was established in 1980 that resulted in the publication titled *Promoting Health/Preventing Disease: Objectives for the Nation.* This report identified 15 priority areas under the headings of preventive services, health protection, and health promotion. These 15 priorities were used to organize 226 objectives that addressed improvements in health status, risk reduction, public and professional awareness, health services and protective measures, and surveillance and evaluation. The objectives were written in specific, quantifiable terms with specific targets to be accomplished by 1990. In 1985, an interim assessment resulted in a 1986 publication titled *The 1990 Health Objectives for the Nation: A Midcourse Review.* Updated objectives appeared in July 1990 and are titled *Promoting Health/Preventing Disease: Year 2000 Objectives for the Nation.*

National Task Force on Eating Disorders

A national task force or consortium for eating disorders among athletes might be modeled after the example presented above. One of the first steps would be to decide on the professional organizations, government agencies, or foundations that might provide financial support. A few possibilities of professional organizations might include the American Alliance for Health, Physical Education, Recreation and Dance (AAHPERD); National Association for Girls and Women in Sport (NAGWS); National Collegiate Athletic Association (NCAA); National Federation of State High School Associations (NFSHSA); American Public Health Association (APHA); American School Health Association (ASHA); American Medical Association (AMA); and the American Heart Association (AHA).

Possible government agencies under the Department of Health and Human Services, Public Health Service (PHS) that might be involved include the Centers for Disease Control; Alcohol, Drug Abuse, and Mental Health Administration; and National Institutes of Health. Other government agencies might include the Department of Education and the National Heart, Blood, and Lung Institution. Additional sources of support might be the President's Council on Physical Fitness and Sports and the National Nutrition Consortium. Possible foundations to support a national task force might be identified by perusing a volume edited by Clinton (1988) titled *National Guide to Foundation Funding in Health.* Corporations and businesses might also be a source of support.

Invitation to National Leaders

Leaders in a number of disciplines should be asked to participate. The focus would be multidisciplinary with a combination of academic and professional people. The professional and academic disciplines that should be represented would be physical education, health promotion and education, communication, psychology, nutrition, nursing, pharmacy, medicine, family studies, sociology, political science, and law. Principally, the representatives would be from the schools of public health, social and behavioral sciences (liberal arts), health sciences, consumer and family science, pharmacy, nursing, law, and medicine. In many instances, subdisciplines would also need to be considered. For example, in physical education significant contributions might be made by those specializing in the philosophy of sport, exercise physiology, biomechanics, athletic training, and intercollegiate athletic administration.

It would also be important to invite representatives from business, media, entertainment, and professional sports. Often celebrities, owners of professional teams, well-known athletes from the past and present, and media executives and broadcasters influence perspectives about sports and the value of athletics in society. Contributions by these individuals might establish or greatly influence the number of possibilities that might be considered as ways to bring about changes.

Issues for the Task Force

There are several issues that might be addressed by the task force. A few of the more salient areas are presented in Table 11.1 and several representative questions appear related to each area. These areas and the questions proposed are not meant to be comprehensive but, hopefully, will serve as an example of areas and issues that need to be addressed. Other issues and questions are expected to be forthcoming from task force sessions.

Task Force Outcomes

Ultimately, the issues that arise would be subdivided into categories. The next step would be to develop measurable objectives for each issue. Several documents could be published to report progress and to modify

Table 11.1

Examples of Areas and Issues to Be Addressed by a Task Force on Eating Disorders Among Athletes

Topic	Question
Society	1. What is the role of athletics in society? 2. What is the purpose of amateur and professional sport? 3. What are acceptable personal and societal performance outcomes of athletics? 4. What should be the perceptions of society about sports? 5. What philosophy or perspective of sport should be emphasized? 6. What would be the goals of athletics from a philosophical/theoretical perspective (e.g., entertainment, leisure)?
Service Providers	1. What is the role of service providers? 2. What interventions for prevention and treatment can be offered by service providers? 3. At what point in athletics should services begin?
Sports Environment	1. What is the role of the coach? 2. What is the role of family and peers? 3. What is the role of media? 4. What is the role of national associations? 5. What is the role of government? 6. What is the role of foundations? 7. What is the role of corporations and business? 8. What is the athlete's responsibility? 9. What is the best way to offer amateur sport opportunities? 10. What measures should be used as an indication of fitness or as qualification requirements to participate?
Related Disciplines	1. What is the role of each of the various disciplines involved? 2. What are future research priorities from a multidisciplinary perspective? 3. What physical, psychological, and sociological factors lead to problems among athletes?

or add to the listed objectives. The exact procedures completed would be contingent upon the model used to develop and operate the task force.

Conclusions

After reading this volume, one is struck with the fact that something needs to be done about the problem of eating disorders among athletes. The question, of course, is what to do? What actions can be taken to alter the seemingly high prevalence of eating disorders among athletes or the anorexic- or bulimic-like attitudes and behaviors and the use of unhealthy weight loss methods? It seems that there are several alternatives, each with advantages and disadvantages. This chapter discussed one of the options. Whether the template, proposed plan, or specific disciplines of attendees presented are correct is really not the issue. The point is that some coordinated broad scale national action needs to take place immediately to set goals and objectives for future research and service. The outcome of a national task force would be not only to increase recognition of the problem but to proceed in an organized and orderly way to, hopefully, eliminate the occurrence of eating disorders and other abuses among athletes.

References

Clinton, J. (Ed.). (1988). *National guide to foundation funding in health*. New York: The Foundation Center.

U.S. Department of Health, Education, and Welfare. (1979). *Healthy people: The Surgeon General's report on health promotion and disease prevention* (DHEW Publication No. 79-55071). Washington, DC: U.S. Government Printing Office.

U.S. Department of Health and Human Services. (1980). *Promoting health/ preventing disease: Objectives for the nation*. Washington, DC: U.S. Government Printing Office.

U.S. Department of Health and Human Services. (1986). *The 1990 health objectives for the nation: A midcourse review*. Washington, DC: U.S. Government Printing Office.

U.S. Department of Health and Human Services. (1990). *Promoting health/ preventing disease: Year 2000 objectives for the nation*. Washington, DC: U.S. Government Printing Office.

Index

Purposes of the American Alliance for Health, Physical Education, Recreation and Dance

The American Alliance is an educational organization, structured for the purposes of supporting, encouraging, and providing assistance to member groups and their personnel throughout the nation as they seek to initiate, develop, and conduct programs in health, leisure, and movement-related activities for the enrichment of human life.

Alliance objectives include:

1. Professional growth and development—to support, encourage, and provide guidance in the development and conduct of programs in health, leisure, and movement-related activities which are based on the needs, interests, and inherent capacities of the individual in today's society.

2. Communication—to facilitate public and professional understanding and appreciation of the importance and value of health, leisure, and movement-related activities as they contribute toward human well-being.

3. Research—to encourage and facilitate research which will enrich the depth and scope of health, leisure, and movement-related activities; and to disseminate the findings to the profession and other interested and concerned publics.

4. Standards and guidelines—to further the continuous development and evaluation of standards within the profession for personnel and programs in health, leisure, and movement-related activities.

5. Public affiars—to coordinate and administer a planned program of professional, public, and governmental relations that will improve education in areas of health, leisure, and movement-related activities.

6. To conduct such other activities as shall be approved by the Board of Governors and the Alliance Assembly, provided that the Alliance shall not engage in any activity which would be inconsistent with the status of an educational and charitable organization as defined in Section 501(c)(3) of the Internal Revenue Code of 1954 or any successor provision thereto, and none of the said purposes shall at any time be deemed or construed to be purposes other than the public benefit purposes and objectives consistent with such educational and charitable status.

Bylaws, Article III